RE-ENTRY

From Military Service To Civilian Employment

By: Keith O. Nyman

Published by: RE-ENTRY
P.O. Box 13535
Portland, Oregon 97213

Copyright © 1981 by Keith O. Nyman

All rights reserved. No part of this book may be reproduced in any form or by any means without the prior written consent of the publisher, excepting brief quotes used in reviews.

Library of Congress Catalog
Card Number: 81-50437

ISBN: 0-9605826-0-6

Printed in the United States of America

Cover design by Dan Burrill

Dedication

This book is dedicated to:

    My Administrative Assistant, Harris Parkell, a U.S. Air Force veteran, in appreciation for his editing skills and for suggesting the title for this book

and

    The United States Navy, in appreciation for a challenging and rewarding career.

    But most of all, this book is for my wife, Joyce, who patiently endures the years until I retire, which probably will be never.

Table of Contents

	Page
CHAPTER 1 - JOB SEARCH	1
PLANNING	2
RESEARCH	2
EXECUTION	3
EXPECTATIONS	3
UNIQUE FEATURES	3
ADDITIONAL INFORMATION	4
SUMMARY	4
CHAPTER 2 - JOB CLASSIFICATION	6
CLASSIFICATIONS	7
TRADITIONAL OCCUPATIONAL CATEGORIES	7
SIMPLIFIED JOB CLASSIFICATION	10
Professional	10
Skilled and Semi-Skilled	13
Unskilled	14
COMPENSATION	15
SUMMARY	16
CHAPTER 3 - 12-9 MONTHS PRE-SEPARATION PLANNING	19
FALSE SECURITY	20
EVALUATION AND RESEARCH	20
EVALUATION OF KNOWLEDGE AND SKILLS	21
DEFINE JOB DUTIES	24
CATEGORIES OF JOB SEARCHERS	26
RESEARCH JOB OPPORTUNITIES	27

MARKET FACTORS	27
Geographical Considerations	28
Family Considerations	28
Demographics	30
Industry Preference	31
Company Size	31
SOURCES OF INFORMATION	32
Libraries	32
State Publications	36
PAST CLASSIFICATION	36
SUMMARY	37
CHAPTER 4 - 9-5 MONTHS PRE-SEPARATION PLANNING	39
FINANCIAL PLANNING	39
How Much Is Enough?	41
CONTINUE RESEARCH	43
DECIDING ALTERNATE CHOICES	44
THE RESUME	45
SUMMARY	45
CHAPTER 5 - 5-2 MONTHS PRE-SEPARATION PLANNING	48
RESEARCH CURRENT INDUSTRY LITERATURE	48
JOIN PROFESSIONAL SOCIETIES	50
PRACTICE INTERVIEW TECHNIQUES	51
JOB SEARCH METHODOLOGIES	51
Resume Distribution	52
Referral Contact	53
Personal Contact	54
Agency Assist	56
BEGIN INDUSTRY CONTACTS	56
THE COVER LETTER	57
SUMMARY	59

CHAPTER 6 - 2-0 MONTHS PRE-SEPARATION PLANNING 61

PREPARE WARDROBE 62
PREPARE "IN PERSON" CONTACT LIST 64
READ THE NEWSPAPERS 66
CONTACT AGENCIES 67
STUDY YOUR CHOSEN PROFESSION/SKILL AREA 67
WORK REFERENCES 67
SUMMARY 68

CHAPTER 7 - THE RESUME 69

PURPOSE OF THE RESUME 69
QUALITY OF THE RESUME 70
   Content of the Resume 72
   Organization of Information 78
   Length of the Resume 79
   Paper Quality 80
   Printing Method 81
RESUME OUTLINE 81
SUMMARY 92

CHAPTER 8 - THE INTERVIEW 94

SUCCESSFUL INTERVIEW TECHNIQUES 95
   Accommodating the Employer 95
   Punctuality 96
   Grooming 96
   Dress 97
   The Employment Application 98
   The Hand Shake 99
   Smoking During Interview 100
   Martini Lunches 100
   Eye Contact 101
   Listening and Talking 102
   Answering Questions 103

Asking Questions	104
Salary Negotiations	105
FOLLOW-UP	106
WHEN THE OFFER IS MADE	106
SUMMARY	107
CHAPTER 9 - SALARY AND BENEFITS	**109**
PRECONCEIVED WORTH	109
SALARY COMPARABILITY	110
YOUR MARKETABILITY	112
THE ART OF NEGOTIATION	114
CONDITIONS FOR NEGOTIATION	115
EXCHANGE INFORMATION	117
LETTER OFFERS	119
SALARY LANGUAGE	120
BENEFITS	120
SUMMARY	125
CHAPTER 10 - PROFIT VS. MISSION	**126**
THE BOTTOM LINE	127
SUMMARY	129
CHAPTER 11 - THE ELEMENTS OF STRESS	**131**
TYPES OF STRESS	132
Emotional	132
Financial	132
Ego	134
Lack of Confidence	135
Loss of Identity	137
SUMMARY	138
CHAPTER 12 - THE RETIREE	**140**
ADVANTAGES	140
Retirement Pay	140

Experience	141
Leadership	141
Survivability	142
Ability to Adapt	142
Work Stability	142
DISADVANTAGES	143
Retirement Pay	143
Age	144
Military Discipline	145
Loyalty and Job Security	145
CHANGING JOBS	147
CHALLENGE AND RESPONSIBILITY	149
DIFFERENT CHALLENGES	152
SUMMARY	154
CHAPTER 13 - AGENCY ASSISTANCE	155
EXPECTATIONS	155
GOVERNMENT AGENCIES	156
PRIVATE EMPLOYMENT AGENCIES	157
Overall Effectiveness	157
Who Pays?	158
Employer's View	159
Applicant's View	161
Selecting An Agency	161
Working With Agencies	164
CAREER COUNSELING FIRMS	167
SUMMARY	169
CHAPTER 14 - STARTING YOUR OWN BUSINESS	171
MOTIVATION AND COMMITMENT	172
THE BUSINESS PLAN	172
Undercapitalization	173
Financial Controls	174
Market Research	177
Expansion	180

FRANCHISES AND DISTRIBUTORSHIPS	181
Franchises	182
Distributorships	184
SUMMARY	188
CHAPTER 15 - THE CASE FOR STAYING IN	190
I SHOULD HAVE	190
HAPPY I DID	191
THE CHOICE IS YOURS	192

Foreword

Keith Nyman has done a great service for future military retirees by putting out this compendium of information on moving into the civilian job market. The book lays out a methodical and orderly approach for the individual to follow so that he can approach this very important phase of his life in an organized way. The book is helpful. It tells where to find information about various corporations and occupations. It is informative. It removes much of the shroud of mystery from the job hunting process and provides practical recommendations to help the retiree enhance his prospects for success. It provides some benchmarks that will be helpful in making relative judgments. It provides an introduction to the art of salary and benefit negotiation. And it is easy and interesting to read.

Mr. Nyman speaks with the authority of experience. He served a full career in the Navy in personnel administration, he has gone through the transition to civilian occupation himself, and for the past several years he has been in the job placement profession observing and assisting literally hundreds of others make the same move. I can think of no better background for an author on such a subject.

There most certainly is a need for a book like this. Although nearly every military retiree moves into some civilian pursuit, the average person finds that he has been so absorbed in his military profession through the years that he really doesn't have a good sense of just how to search out job opportunities and make judgments on his relative worth in the job market. If he doesn't pursue a learning process in a fairly organized way, he is very apt to miss opportunities, undervalue his worth, and perhaps make his life miserable by accepting employment for which he really has no motivation simply to have a job.

Unfortunately, one of the few things military service does <u>not</u> prepare you to do is to market yourself for employment. For all the bad things we've all said and felt about military personnel systems, they are, in fact, pretty well organized at doing most of the job of placing you in a particular occupation and a particular location for you. Not so in the civilian world. Oh, you can take aptitude tests and courses on how to write resumes and cope with job interviews, but you will pay an expensive price for the experience and will still find that all that preparation won't guarantee you a job. In the final analysis, finding the job falls on your shoulders, and the more effort and thought you put into it, the more likely you are to find something that really meets all your needs and objectives. This book will definitely help you organize your thoughts and should answer a lot of questions on your mind. Above all, it removes a lot of the mystique from the subject and gives practical advice on getting on with the business at hand. I recommend it highly.

       Robert B. Baldwin
       Vice Admiral, U.S. Navy (Retired)

Chapter 1

JOB SEARCH

INTRODUCTION

The separating military person is faced with a special set of problems when he enters the civilian job market. Regardless of his term of service, he will find he has lost contact with the job market. He faces the necessity to evaluate his military experience by matching the things he has learned and done to civilian job requirements.

The entire procedure of job search is probably a mystery to him. He attempts to formulate plans for a job search but is unable to find information which relates to his situation. There are so many aspects to a good job search that he may spend hours of research in order to find information on only selected topics. Nowhere, it seems, is there one publication that contains all of the information he needs to help prepare himself for the search.

Military personnel usually leave the service with little understanding of the job market. At best they have a fragmented plan of action to secure employment. This book attempts to help both present and former military personnel find their way in the civilian job market through good job search techniques.

PLANNING

Planning is vital to a successful job search. In a planned search you must think, evaluate, research, and direct your efforts to pre-determined targets. Timing will become an important part of your plan. Job search techniques include, among other things, preparation of a resume, preparing yourself for the interview, understanding salary negotiations, as well as knowing about places where you may be able to get assistance.

With a good plan you can enhance your chances of not only finding a job, but finding the "right" job in a far shorter time than you could without a plan.

If you do plan to separate from military service, the countdown for your activities begins at minus 12 months. There is a lot of work to be done to make the transition go smoothly. Beginning one year before your discharge is not rushing into it. The people who have elected to not serve in the military have a running start on you in the race toward getting good civilian jobs. The procedures for a successful job search outlined in this book have been written to help ensure that you not only keep pace with them, but that you win the race!

RESEARCH

There is no way to escape the necessity of doing research in a good, planned job search. The job market is so vast that you must identify only those portions of it which will receive your attention. Otherwise, your efforts will be too scattered to do a proper search.

You must seek out details of companies, products or services, and latest trends in industry to prepare yourself for the search. The research won't be easy but you will be well rewarded for the time and effort put forth in that portion of the plan.

EXECUTION

The execution phase of your plan will begin the exciting portion of your job search. Your actions should be well timed and directed. You frequently will be thankful that you took the time and made the effort to do proper research. You will possess valuable knowledge which will enable you to approach an interview with far greater confidence than if you did a haphazard or shortcut job of planning and research.

During execution of your plan, you will have the assurance that you are directing your efforts toward those opportunities which will most satisfy your desires. You will have options to exercise which will give you flexibility in your search.

EXPECTATIONS

In a planned job search your expectations more closely match reality than in an unplanned search. A planned search forces you to face reality. This is extremely important since by not facing reality you reduce your effectiveness in job search. When your expectations exceed reality, you are capable of passing up the best opportunities available for you.

UNIQUE FEATURES

There are many, many features of job search techniques that most job searchers never consider in a search plan. There are some unique features that you, as a former military person, must consider in addition to those features other job searchers must evaluate. These unique features have to do with the perceptions employers have about your military experience and service. Understanding and reacting properly to the employer's perceptions about you will enable you to combat some prejudices they may have about military service.

ADDITIONAL INFORMATION

The chapters of this book contain additional information that is related to job search and, as a whole, will help broaden your outlook on civilian business and employment. The information is included for the reason that any information relevant to civilian business is valuable information to you. Your efforts up to now have been devoted to military service which has occupied your time and thoughts. All the help you can get to re-orient your thinking to civilian employment will serve you well in your search.

SUMMARY

Planning and research are essential for a successful, timely job search. The search plan you prepare and execute will give direction to your efforts. If your expectations are in line with reality, you can recognize a good opportunity when you find one. Certain unique features of job search will be used by former military personnel. They will help the employer understand your military experience. The more you understand civilian business, the more confident you will be in your job search.

ENCOURAGEMENT

The fact that you are concerned enough about understanding job search to read this book improves the odds that you will realize your potential in civilian employment.

Chapter 2

JOB CLASSIFICATION

INTRODUCTION

"How do I go about finding a job?" "What kind of job should I look for?"

Equally difficult as these questions is the logical sequence for topics for discussion which answer them. The civilian business world is a different place from the one in which you've been recently, and the longer you've been away from it, the more alien it will seem when you put yourself on the job market.

Being a military person, you are probably accustomed to facing the situation "head-on," so let's do just that. After we get some sort of handle on the market, we'll tackle the planning aspects of a job search. After that, we will consider those things that could impact on your plan and plan accordingly. Some of the subjects we will discuss are items you should have thought of or known about already. Other subjects are of a nature which clearly should be in your bank of knowledge when job searching, but no one has addressed them in that context. The reasons for some of the things we discuss no one knows. But these things are considered important in the civilian business world and knowing about them will help you.

Over the years there have been various trends in what constitutes job satisfaction. During the economic depression of the 1930's just being employed was job satisfaction. In the late 1960's and early 1970's the job had to be fulfilling to be satisfying. The latter was a societal trend but the emphasis was correct. Whatever job makes you the happiest, regardless of title, and enables you to earn a living within the bounds of the law and morality is what you should try to find. No one is going to live your life for you.

CLASSIFICATIONS

First, we will address job classification in the more traditional sense, that is by occupational category. Then we will take a more simplified, albeit arbitrary, approach to job classification. The reason we will do this is so we can adapt it to a consideration probably more important to most job searchers than the traditional method of classification. That consideration is the perceived social status or "pecking order" of jobs. That way we can cross occupational lines and perhaps satisfy some questions you may have regarding job titles and what are reasonable experience, responsibility or authority levels for job titles. This arbitrary method of classification, therefore, attempts to address the job market in a way which is not normally done, but to which people seem to relate to more and more as time goes by.

TRADITIONAL OCCUPATIONAL CATEGORIES

The various traditional occupational categories are as follows:

- Professional, Technical and Managerial Occupations

  These are concerned with such fields as art, science, engineering, education, medicine, law, business relations, and administrative, managerial, and technical work

- Clerical and Sales Occupations

    These fields are concerned with preparing, transcribing, transferring, systematizing, and preserving written communications and records; collecting accounts; distributing information; and influencing customers in favor of a commodity or service.

- Service Occupations

    Concerned with performing tasks in and around private households; serving individuals in institutions and in commercial and other establishments; and protecting the public against crime, fire, accidents, and acts of war.

- Farming, Fishery, Forestry, and Related Occupations

    These fields are mainly involved with growing, harvesting, catching, and gathering land and aquatic plant and animal life and the products thereof, and with providing services in support of these activities.

- Processing Occupations

  Primarily concerned with refining, mixing, compounding, chemically treating, heat treating, or similarly working materials and products.

- Machine Trades Occupations

  Concerned with feeding, tending, operating, controlling, and setting up machines to cut, bore, mill, abrade, print, and similarly work such materials as metal, paper, wood and stone.

- Bench Work Occupations

  Concerned with the use of handtools and bench machines to fit, grind, carve, mold, paint, sew, assemble, inspect, repair, and similarly work relatively small objects and materials.

- Structural Work Occupations

  These occupations involve fabricating, erecting, installing, paving, painting, repairing, and similarly working structures or structural parts.

- Miscellaneous Occupations

  This category is concerned with transportation services; packaging and warehousing; utilities; amusement, recreation, and motion picture services; mining and logging; graphic arts; and various miscellaneous activities.

SIMPLIFIED JOB CLASSIFICATION

In the following simplified view of job classification we will essentially ignore traditional occupational categories and industry designations and view job classification more in terms of responsibility, knowledge, experience, and authority levels. Basically, we will classify jobs into three categories or markets. They are:

- Professional
- Skilled or Semi-skilled
- Unskilled

A discussion of each category is worthwhile since it may help you determine where you **may** fit.

Professional

The professional market is the most difficult to define. Why? One reason is because of the advances in scientific technology and management sciences. Another is because any job clearly not in the skilled trades, semi-skilled, or unskilled classifications has somehow, in the minds of most people, been elevated to being a "position," and, consequently, in the category of "professional employment." It seems a "job" is not good enough anymore. All sorts of euphemistic titles clutter organizational charts for positions but when examined at the functional level they are, after-all, jobs.

The entire professional market has to a good degree been modified to accommodate those people who want positions as opposed to jobs. If the distinction is important to you, stick with it. It is an established fact that people will often work harder and for less money if they have a title which connotes position in society than they will in a job which provides the best working conditions or more money. The employer is happy to attach a fine title to a job which pays poorly for the work and responsibility involved in order to get the best qualified person who has a hang-up about title.

Out of the tens of thousands of titles for jobs in the civilian job market you can find numerous variations for positioning that job on an organizational chart. Private business is not restrained to following the dictates of an ultimate authority which controls such things. It is sometimes even more difficult to understand that the same title encompasses altogether different duties in different organizations. Confusing? You bet. That's why titles can be very misleading.

Generally speaking, it is quite safe to categorize professional positions as those that:

- Have P&L (Profit and Loss) responsibility;

- Are heading up a line or staff function;

- Are in a significant position of leadership, management, or supervision;

- Require a high degree of education or technical knowledge; and/or

- Are in a function which demands extraordinary personality traits. For example, sales work at certain levels would enjoy professional status classification.

Are the above classifications arbitrary? Certainly they are, but they do provide some general guidelines for classification of jobs by level of responsibility and authority.

About the word "professional" — it is a handy word with which even Webster has some trouble. A person can be a professional anything -- but is it, in reality, a profession? One good way to determine if a job is in the realm of professionals is if the person is engaged in one of the learned professions; that is, a position usually requiring a significant amount of college education. The very word professional has been so overused as to give added prestige to jobs of every classification.

We are reminded at this point of those engaged in what is referred to as "the world's oldest profession." It is obvious by the young ages of some that a significant amount of education was not necessary to achieve their positions. So it may be concluded that the word "professional," in some cases, is used only to convey a dignity that otherwise may be missing because of the nature of the work or because of the employee's concept of it.

Some newspapers have the courage to list jobs under the title of professional, skilled, etc. If you read some of the ads, you will see that few job titles are the sacrosanct domain of a given profession.

Real confusion enters the picture when you consider all the entry level positions of management. At just what point in time or development does an entry level person become a professional? See the problem? There is no clear cut answer.

We run into similar problems with titles such as "Manager" and "Supervisor." If there were some common denominator which we could cite to strictly classify these jobs, our task would be easier. For the purpose of this discussion, these titles will be considered to fall under the category of professional since they generally are considered to be in the upper reaches of pecking order as far as jobs and titles go.

Perhaps the most important thing to you should be that you are comfortable with a given title — if that's what you want.

Skilled and Semi-Skilled

The skilled and semi-skilled markets are generally associated with either the trades, e.g., electricians, plumbers, carpenters, masons, pipefitters, etc., or clerical occupations. For the most part, labor unions have done a splendid job of monopolizing trade occupations. If you plan to enter the trades, it is a good idea to go to your base library and study unionism. Terms like Union Shop, Closed Shop, Open Shop, etc., are all part of lengthy and complex labor agreements. A basic knowledge of these will help you fight the red tape when striving to get a job where a union is well entrenched.

Unaccustomed as the military person is to union activity, an understanding of how unions work will give you an insight into what to expect if you become a member of a union. The best indicator one can find of whether a union is successful or unsuccessful is in the pay, benefits, and treatment that employees receive. The unions need a platform to succeed. Remove the platform and they are unsuccessful. If you work in a non-union shop, you can usually expect less pay and poorer benefits than in a union shop.

There are many skilled jobs in the civilian job market which require a great deal of ability and/or knowledge. It is a safe bet that if it is a sizeable market, a union has captured it or has targeted the jobs for unionization. Clerical jobs, for example, have recently been subjected to heavy union organization drives.

The best advice that can be given to anyone joining a unionized company is this: **Read the contract carefully and put in a good day's work.** There are no free lunches.

Any person who has attended a military school in a specialized area should, at the least, enter the skilled or semi-skilled market. You have received some of the finest training available anywhere — put it to use. Even if you received no specialized training, the fact you were accepted in the military and satisfactorily completed your enlistment separates you from most unskilled workers. You've stuck out a job for 3, 4 or more years under adverse conditions! Many unskilled people cannot or will not hold a job for any length of time.

Unskilled

The unskilled market is vast and varied. Unskilled labor, or common labor as it is often called, usually requires little education. Repetitive tasks on production lines are typical of unskilled jobs. Upward mobility from the unskilled ranks is possible but far too few companies provide the training or opportunity to accomplish it.

If the person's education or capabilities are limited, they can find satisfaction in this type of work and their contribution is very necessary to industry. Until they gain seniority on the job, however, their job security can be tenuous.

Responsibility in unskilled jobs is often restricted to meeting production norms established for the job. The established norms are designed to gain maximum productivity from the employee. If the company utilizes industrial engineers to study the job, they can usually find the easiest and most efficient way the job should be performed.

Union representation is well entrenched in the unskilled market. This representation, when present, usually provides for better wages and benefits.

If you are content in an unskilled job, that's fine. Stick with it and do a good job. If the employer has any sense about him, you will be respected and appreciated.

COMPENSATION

If you have been in the military for 6-10 years or more, be aware that salaries and benefits for jobs have undergone a very significant evolution. White collar professional jobs no longer are the exclusive domain of the higher paid. The skilled and semi-skilled trades have in many cases far outstripped many professional classification jobs in pay. In the trades, $10.00, $15.00, and $17.00 an hour and more are common. Using a standard industry formula of 2080 hours in a work year, you can compute some handsome salaries. For example:

$15.00 per hr. X 2080 hrs. = $31,200.00

That's straight time! Most tradesmen work some overtime at time-and-a-half pay under union contracts. How does that compare with the "executive" or "management" salary? Most degreed entry level through mid-level managers have real trouble rationalizing this anomaly of salaries.

The benefit packages of unionized skilled tradesmen are unbeatable. Management often has a tough time keeping management's benefits on a par with union benefits much less surpassing them. These benefits are very expensive. Don't be too surprised if you find management on the short end of the stick in benefits. If you're in management and find yourself in such a situation, your job title just might make the situation palatable.

You can compare this situation of pay evolution to critical shortage pay, variable re-enlistment bonuses and the other special programs for more pay in the military. It is the old law of supply and demand in action. Generally speaking, the same shortages of skills the military experiences are simply a mirror of what's available to the private employer. There is premium pay for skills in short supply. Only the variances in pay are greater in the civilian market because there is no rank structure restricting basic pay to a mere 26 levels as in the military. Business exercises more flexibility in pay because it is one of their best weapons in completing their mission which is singular in purpose and well defined — PROFIT. They will use any weapon at their disposal to reach that goal.

SUMMARY

The foregoing view of classification of the civilian job market is an extremely simplified treatment of the subject. Entire volumes have been written about the subject. The <u>Dictionary of Occupational Titles,</u> for example, contains tens of thousands of job titles and descriptions under most precise classifications. To the uninitiated, it is confusing; to the competent personnel classifiers, it is a tool to bring some order to their profession.

The civilian job market is so vast and complex that it is best to approach it with a simplified view of classification. Where you fit into the scheme of things regarding classification of your job can be of importance to you. Just don't let classification cloud your perspective and send you on a wild goose chase. Classification is only one aspect of the job. Look for the full meaning. Your job search will be much more effective.

ENCOURAGEMENT

Most civilians have a poorer understanding of job classifications than you. The military has one of the best systems there is. Classification or title doesn't make the person. You still have to do the job.

PRE-SEPARATION

PLANNING AND RESEARCH CHART

Chapter 3 12-9 Months Prior	Chapter 4 9-5 Months Prior	Chapter 5 5-2 Months Prior	Chapter 6 2-0 Months Prior
Evaluation of Knowledge and Skills	Financial Planning	Research Current Industry Literature	Prepare Wardrobe
Define Job Duties	Continue Research	Join Professional Societies	Prepare "In Person" Contact List
Research Job Opportunities	Decide Alternate Choices	Practice Interview Techniques	Read Newspapers
Determine Your Market Factors from list below:	Prepare Resume	Formulate Search Methods	Contact Agencies
–Geographic Areas –Family Considerations –Demographics –Industry Preference –Company Size		Begin Industry Contacts	Study Your Chosen Professional/Skill Area Obtain Work Reference Letter from Superior
Research Sources of Information			

Chapter 3

12-9 MONTHS PRE-SEPARATION PLANNING

INTRODUCTION

Almost without exception there is no reason an ex-military person has to be long on the job market. The training, knowledge, and skills the separating military person possesses are in demand in civilian industry.

You should be working within 30 to 60 days. If you find yourself on the job market much longer than 90 days, you will start to wonder if your planning was faulty or your goals unrealistic. One or both reasons probably will be the case.

What the separating military person does not have is solid, up-to-date knowledge of the job market and job search techniques. Both of these shortcomings can be overcome by planning and research. A well thought out and executed plan can reduce the anxieties accompanying a search and bring results in a timely manner which are in concert with your goals and expectations.

If you are uncertain over what type of job you will search for, start your planning and research nine months to a year before you separate.

Nine months to one year before your separation is not too soon to start planning. If you are certain of what you want to do and have prior knowledge of that market, you can let your planning be delayed for some months.

FALSE SECURITY

If you are depending on contacts in your market to help you land a job, do not be lulled into complacency and a false sense of security. Talk is cheap, commitment is real. Commitment isn't there until a start date is firmly established and **all** the necessary negotiations for salary and benefits are completed. Even then, if the start date is more than 45 days away, you had better have some sort of alternate plan handy. Too many things can happen in private business over a few short months which can alter the best of intentions as regards employment promises. It takes a very secure business with very critical needs to make commitments any length of time in the future. The largest companies will hedge their promise because they usually have a good flow of applicants. Why promise something today for six months ahead when there is more than a fair chance someone more qualified will apply in the interim?

EVALUATION AND RESEARCH

Your pre-separation planning will require a great deal of evaluation and research if you're to do it correctly. Any person attempting job search without evaluating their knowledge, skill, and training, may find it difficult to identify their market. You cannot escape the necessity to research the job market in pre-separation planning. Research will enable you to direct your job search efforts properly.

EVALUATION OF KNOWLEDGE AND SKILLS

The evaluation portion of pre-separation planning consists of a hard look at the knowledge and skills you possess. If you feel you can articulate your skills and knowledge with five minutes of thought, you're going to have a tough time convincing an employer of your worth.

The best way you can start to evaluate your knowledge and skills is by making a list of them. If you have difficulty in compiling such a list it is all the more important that you take the time to complete it. You may be able to tell a fellow serviceman in the same service your rank, job title, M.O.S., N.E.C., or A.F.S.C, and he will understand perfectly your knowledge and skills. Tell the same thing to a civilian employer and you'll get a reaction you weren't expecting — complete ignorance of your background.

Don't be alarmed. Each of us tends to evaluate things in the perspective of our own experience and knowledge. You will be fortunate if the employer is ex-military, particularly from your branch of service. He will have some understanding of your knowledge and skills. Even if the employer is ex-military his information may be dated, which is something better than no knowledge at all of military skills.

In private business there is a decided tendency to view experiences in the perspective of their industry, their discipline, their specific product line, etc. A good job candidate will know how to get around these biases. It isn't easy.

When you list your knowledge and skills use universal terms to describe leadership roles, staff functions, teaching roles, and equipment operated or worked on. Start getting accustomed to using universal terms for the things you do by phasing out your usage of military terms. This will put you in a better position to discuss your background in terms with which business people are familiar. When you list a skill or knowledge, list additional subtopics which more fully explain the leading term. Again, use universal terms whenever possible. In reality what you will be doing is making an inventory of your skills and knowledge. Such an inventory will reinforce your memory in an interview situation.

If this sounds trite, like a waste of time, try this. Right now, without consulting your organization manual, write a complete job description for your job. How long did it take you to write it? Did you hesitate in what to include? Did you hesitate in selecting the words you should use in explaining your job?

Most first employment interviews are brief affairs which only serve to separate the wheat from the chaff. It may be your only chance to say it and to say it right — so make it count. With a complete inventory of your skills and knowledge on your mind or at your finger tips, you'll stand a lot better chance to get them into your interview discussions.

If you hesitated in selecting the words you should use in explaining your job, you may have anticipated the problem you could run into. Ask the question, "If a civilian employer completely unfamiliar with the military were to read my list, would he then know what I do?" The point is, you know what you're doing but you may be using a foreign language in trying to tell that civilian employer what it is.

Now comes the hard part to accept. You don't have the time to educate that civilian to your language. Furthermore, he doesn't even want to try to learn it. He may not be smart enough to learn it. However, it becomes a problem for you -- not for him.

Some publications advise ex-military to "civilianize" their resume. On the surface this sounds good, but one simple question by the employer will blow your cover. That question is, "Where did you do all this -- with what company?" You have no choice but to tell him, "In the military." You will never be able to hide the fact you were in the military. To completely civilianize your resume smacks of evasion of facts. You don't have a thing to apologize for, so don't start doing it with your resume. (To help you in the preparation of the resume, Chapter 7 is devoted entirely to the topic.)

You can use universal terms to summarize your duties, responsibilities, authority, skills, and knowledge while still stating clearly that it was in a military command. Your military experience has a comparable civilian **application** even though it is not experience in a civilian organization.

In listing your skills and knowledge do so separately for each job you've had in the military. If there is no universal term which applies, keep the military term. Every job has certain unique aspects for which only one term applies. Just be prepared to elaborate on it's meaning.

Now you have a complete inventory of what you have done in the military. Congratulations! You've completed your first phase of planning. Now you should start your first phase of research.

DEFINE JOB DUTIES

From your inventory of knowledge and skills select those which gave you the most satisfaction while attaining or performing them. One of the best indicators of what you will enjoy most and be best at in the future are those which you enjoyed doing and were good at in the past. There are few jobs which have no favorable aspects to the person performing them. If you're having trouble with the listing, examine subcomponents of the duties and knowledge. Don't worry about the length of the list; the more the better.

Job duties I would **most** like to perform (taken from your list of knowledge gained and skills performed during your service):

1.

2.

3.

What you are looking for is a trend. You may end up with several trends. That's fine because it gives you options. If you can't find a job in your first choice of options, then the second or third choices are likely candidates.

Job exploration may be fun but it can be costly and stressful. If you can identify those things you like to do and find a job which satisfies them, your chances of success are enhanced considerably.

Once you have identified the trend or trends of things you have enjoyed doing the most begin arranging them in job description format. In other words, you now have the opportunity to write your own description of the job you would most like to have. From the trends you selected you may be able to write several job descriptions. Some military jobs have no direct civilian counterparts but don't let that alarm you. If you disregard title and look at the basic elements of your military job or specialty you can be assured there are counterpart duties, skills, or knowledge required in civilian jobs. They may go by a different name or encompass only a portion of them, but there are counterparts.

If you are having trouble writing a job description, you can really "pin down" what you're after by researching the Dictionary of Occupational Titles. If you can't find a job description in the D.O.T. that suits your desires, you're in trouble. That publication is so vast and diverse in job descriptions that it is difficult to conceive your niche isn't listed there somewhere. The D.O.T. has the advantage of listing jobs by occupation. Once you've identified the occupational field, it helps to identify the industry or type of company for which you would want to work.

Once you have one or more proposed job descriptions written down, ask yourself the following questions:

- Which industry or industries are most likely to utilize people with this job description?

- What size company most likely will employ someone with this job description?

Answering these questions may be difficult at this point in time. You should be able to answer these questions easily once you have completed the necessary research.

CATEGORIES OF JOB SEARCHERS

There are three general categories of job searchers:

- First are the ones who know exactly what they want to do and will hold out until they find it. That's fine if you have a highly marketable skill and know your market. These people still should prepare an alternate plan for a fallback position.

- In the second category are those people who have a specific industry in mind with a number of possible positions within that industry as targets. They, too, should have an alternate plan ready for use should they fail in their search.

- In the third category are the people who have no clear idea of the job or the industry in which they want to work. They have the greatest amount of research to do and initial decision making to face.

We shall discuss the research phase by addressing the last category listed. This is appropriate since the entire idea of job research is to focus your attention to a manageable and limited market.

RESEARCH JOB OPPORTUNITIES

In approaching the first phase of research you should select a target or perhaps several targets. If you have a firm commitment in your own mind as to what job and industry you want to work in, your research will be somewhat simplified. If you really have no idea what you want to do except in general "find a good job," then you had better start doing some serious thinking. The odds are solidly against a job finding you. So think about what you want to do while you have the time and a steady paycheck. Employers are quick to perceive a person in desperate need of a job and will react accordingly. Don't let lack of planning eat up time and resources and place you in that position.

MARKET FACTORS

For the moment forget about pay, title, benefits and similar factors. It is far more important to live where you want to, work in the industry you want, doing the things (duties) you like to do, in the size company you feel you'll be comfortable in, than how much money you'll be making. Money is rarely the prime factor in job satisfaction. Look at any study conducted by industrial psychologists and you will see that factors like challenge, job duties, and working environment are invariably listed before salary as the most important factor in a job. Job security is fast becoming a very important factor to most people. Anyone who has been laid off from a job will quickly list job security as their prime consideration in their next job.

There may be some job factors that are very important to you which you may want to include in selecting your market. Just be aware that each additional factor you add is restricting your market. Get too "nit-picking" and you'll reduce your options to unemployment.

Geographical Considerations

When you choose an industry and company of a particular size, make sure that the geographic area will support those choices. You would be surprised how many people harbor a desire for a specific geographic location, industry, or size of company other than what they have, but absolutely refuse to sacrifice one criterion for the other. They live in a perpetual dream world which will never be fulfilled short of taking the action necessary to realize it — namely, a move. Don't make the mistake of getting caught up in that dream world. Make the trade-off now, early in the game, and live with the decision. At least you'll have comfort in knowing that you had the facts when you made the decision.

Family Considerations

Family ties are strong. If proximity to relatives is a must for you or your family, be prepared to sacrifice job satisfaction if necessary. Make that decision early in your planning phase. It will save a lot of arguments and enable you to intelligently research viable alternatives in terms of industry or job desired. It's miserable enough to be unemployed. To be unemployed and somewhere your family detests increases the potential for domestic troubles. You would be wise to involve your family in your decision. They will be more likely to be supportive of your final decision on where you will live and work if they had an opportunity to give their input.

Too many ex-military people who are unfamiliar with their market choice throw their efforts to the wind. They become disillusioned when the realization hits them that there is no market, or a limited market for their skills in their preferred geographic location. Too late they realize they must settle for second, third, or last choice in order to get a job.

An analogy to this situation is the serviceman who always wanted that duty in Sweden, or Butte, Montana. He keeps listing them as a choice for a duty station but there just was no job available for his skills in those places. If he would have bothered to check that out first, he could have saved the choice for a duty station that was attainable and not wasted his efforts. He may have gotten Hawaii instead of the only "available" billet in Adak, Alaska. The person who made the assignment didn't see a viable "choice" to which he could be assigned and therefore assigned him to whatever was available.

Geographic area(s) in which my family and I would want to live:

1.

2.

3.

Geographic area(s) in which my family and I would live for the right job:

1.

2.

3.

Demographics

Once you have chosen the geographic location(s) you would live in, and taken into account family desires, create another list. This time you will be considering the demographics of the area. If the area is in or near large population centers, you increase your market potential. If you're going to get away from it all and live in a remote area or in a small town, you may have to settle for something less than your first choice for industry and job duties. Be realistic. If you want to be a helicopter mechanic, you won't have very good job hunting in places like Plains, Georgia; Caldwell, Idaho; or Truth Or Consequences, New Mexico. Industry supports population and vice versa. If population supports the industry of your choice, go where the greatest number of opportunities are available, e.g., large population areas.

Population of areas in which I want to live:

1.

2.

3.

Population of area(s) in which I would live for the right job:

1.

2.

3.

When you have narrowed your geographic choice(s) down to places where you want to live, for whatever reason, your next task is to research the industry in which you want to work. Some industries are everywhere. Service industries, hospitality (hotel, motel, restaurants), etc., are everywhere in varying degrees of volume. Manufacturing as a broad classification is most everywhere. Other industries are regional in nature such as agricultural. The point is, do your research to determine to what extent your industry choice is located in your geographic preference.

It may be that your industry choice will take precedence over your geographic preference. Only you can make that decision. Your research will enable you to identify which industries are in your geographic choices.

Industry Preference

Industry(ies) in which I would most like to work:

1.

2.

3.

Company Size

Some people feel like a fish out of water in the wrong size company. While one person will feel his promotion opportunities are enhanced in a large company, another will feel he will never be able to ascend to the top ranks because of the competition. The same holds true on people's feelings about medium size or small companies. Some view large companies as being more secure, but this may not be the case. Some people feel "lost in the crowd" in a large company and feel comfortable in a small one. In summary, only you, as an individual can decide what size of company you prefer. However, be aware that size of company can be very misleading in terms of general, and certainly specific, expectations. In the final analysis, you will never know for sure what to expect until you join that company.

Size of company I'd like to work for:

Rank in order of preference:

Large   ___

Medium ___

Small   ___

SOURCES OF INFORMATION

Libraries

Your best sources of information for research purposes on industries are in large public libraries. You will be absolutely amazed at the number of industrial directories they house. To name a few, there is the Million Dollar Directory published by Dun & Bradstreet. It lists by geographic area, as well as type of industry, thousands of companies which do a million dollars or more in business a year. The Metal Working Directory, also published by Dun & Bradstreet, lists thousands of businesses from the smallest to the largest by geographic location -- right down to county and city. Each of these publications have names, addresses, phone numbers, products, etc., listed for each company.

In the Dun and Bradstreet directories, as well as the vast majority of other directories, information on companies is classified by S.I.C. codes. S.I.C. stands for Standard Industrial Classification. The S.I.C. code is basically a product code. They are all four digit codes derived from two digit major grouping codes. They are organized as follows:

Major Group 20 - Food and Kindred Products
21 Tobacco Manufacturers
22 Textile Mill Products
23 Apparel and Other Finished Products Made From Fabrics and Similar Materials
24 Lumber and Wood Products, Except Furniture
25 Furniture and Fixtures
26 Paper and Allied Products
27 Printing, Publishing, and Allied Industries
28 Chemicals and Allied Products
29 Petroleum Refining and Related Industries
30 Rubber and Miscellaneous Plastics Products
31 Leather and Leather Products
32 Stone, Clay, Glass, and Concrete Products
33 Primary Metal Industries
34 Fabricated Metal Products, Except Machinery and Transportation Equipment
35 Machinery, Except Electrical
36 Electrical and Electronic Machinery, Equipment, and Supplies
37 Transportation Equipment

38 Measuring, Analyzing, and Controlling Instruments; Photographic, Medical, and Optical Goods, Watches and Clocks

39 Miscellaneous Manufacturing Industries

Within each Major Group are numerous subdivisions and subdivision titles. Examples:

361 Electric Transmission and Distribution Equipment

362 Electrical Industrial Apparatus

363 Household Appliances

364 Electrical Lighting and Wiring Equipment

These, then, are refined further into four digit codes representing specific products:

3612 Power, Distribution, and Specialty Transformers
3613 Switchgear and Switchboard Apparatus

3621 Motors and Generators
3622 Industrial Controls
3623 Welding Apparatus, Electric
3624 Carbon and Graphite Products
3629 Electrical Industrial Apparatus, Not Elsewhere Classified

3631 Household Cooking Equipment
3632 Household Refrigerators and Home and Farm Freezers
3633 Household Laundry Equipment

3634 Electric Housewares and Fans
3635 Household Vacuum Cleaners
3636 Sewing Machines
3639 Household Appliances, Not Elsewhere Classified

3641 Electric Lamps
3643 Current Carrying Wiring Devices
3644 Noncurrent Carrying Wiring Devices
3645 Residential Electric Lighting Fixtures
3646 Commercial, Industrial and Institutional Electric Lighting Fixtures
3647 Vehicular Lighting Equipment
3648 Lighting Equipment, Not Elsewhere Classified

As you can see, there is a good probability that your skills and knowledge can be utilized in industries listed in these directories. When you consider there are directories for most industries, there is a tremendous amount of information available to you that can assist you in selecting target companies.

You will find directories for hundreds of industries including electronics, food processing, mining, plastics, chemicals, etc., ad infinitum. What a gold mine for the job searcher!

Also in large public libraries you will find directories listing the officers and membership of professional societies. There are trade journals of every description. There is the Thomas Register with its numerous volumes giving you information on thousands upon thousands of companies, industries, and products.

State Publications

Most states publish industrial directories for their state. In order to receive a copy, write to the Secretary of State in the state(s) you have targeted for your job search. The Secretary of State, in turn, will channel your request to the appropriate department. These publications will cost you from $10.00 to about $150.00. They are worth their weight in gold, though, to the job hunter. Most large public libraries carry them for their state and neighboring states.

PAST CLASSIFICATION

For the size of American industry one would think there would be numerous, large, efficient job counseling and classification centers. In truth, the various agencies doing the task fall far short of expectations. We shall address this problem in a later chapter. You will be well advised to take advantage of any pre-separation career counseling offered by the military. Be assured that the initial classification you had in the military was probably the best you'll ever experience. Overall, the proficiency the military has in job classification and placement of their people is far superior to that which is generally found in civilian industry. Civilians are essentially left to their own devices to find their niche. It is a fact neither high schools, universities, nor industry do as good a job in job counseling and classification as does the military. That is why your research is so important. Be prepared to do it for yourself in a job search. You will be fortunate indeed if someone does it for you.

SUMMARY

The purpose of your research of civilian industries is to gather as much information as you can about your market. No one is going to hand this information to you on a silver platter, you have to dig for it. Work? You bet it is. Effective? Only if you use the information.

If you discipline yourself and accomplish the planning and research steps recommended in this chapter you will have a good idea of what kind of job you should look for and which industry or industries can utilize your skills and knowledge. It's a lot of work but if you really want to have the edge on the employment game, it's a necessary exercise.

If you concentrate your efforts in the proper direction, you will be effective in a job search. Nine to 12 months before separation is not too early to start laying the groundwork for an effective search. An effective search requires that you be aware of many factors in the employment game. Foremost among these factors involves knowing what you're looking for and where you can find it. You should now have a good idea of what and where. How you go about finding that job will be easier now that you really know what you're looking for.

ENCOURAGEMENT

You have skills and knowledge that are in demand in civilian industry. You will find the job you're looking for through good planning and research.

PRE-SEPARATION

PLANNING AND RESEARCH CHART

Chapter 3 12-9 Months Prior	**Chapter 4** **9-5 Months Prior**	Chapter 5 5-2 Months Prior	Chapter 6 2-0 Months Prior
Evaluation of Knowledge and Skills	**Financial Planning**	Research Current Industry Literature	Prepare Wardrobe
Define Job Duties	**Continue Research**	Join Professional Societies	Prepare "In Person" Contact List
Research Job Opportunities	**Decide Alternate Choices**	Practice Interview Techniques	Read Newspapers
Determine Your Market Factors from list below:	**Prepare Resume**	Formulate Search Methods	Contact Agencies
-Geographic Areas -Family Considerations -Demographics -Industry Preference -Company Size		Begin Industry Contacts	Study Your Chosen Professional/Skill Area
Research Sources of Information			Obtain Work Reference Letter from Superior

38

Chapter 4

9-5 MONTHS PRE-SEPARATION PLANNING

INTRODUCTION

If you have just begun your planning and research, there still is sufficient time to do a thorough job. However, it shouldn't be put off any longer. Time passes so fast that priorities in your work and other pre-separation planning will eat into the time reserved for job search.

Under the chapter entitled "The Elements of Stress," the elements of financial stress are given heavy emphasis. The necessity of financial planning is a factor for which many people do not have a proper respect until it is too late. During the 9-5 month period prior to your separation from the military you would be wise to evaluate your financial condition and plan accordingly. Financial planning, along with the other recommended planning actions in this chapter, will pay handsome dividends when you place yourself on the job market.

FINANCIAL PLANNING

Each of us has a marvelous capacity for spending money. With each commitment to spending we somehow manage to take on more debt than could be immediately satisfied if the demand for full payment were made. From a very young age, we have been firmly indoctrinated in the workings of a consumer society. The ability to consume is easy. The financial capacity to support consumption at the level we desire is the hard part to achieve.

"Success" to a majority of Americans, means that one is able to consume more. An American's freedom to consume is so closely associated with his concept of success that his financial capacity is often used as a measure of success.

The necessity for money in our lives is something we cannot ignore. How we relate to it can have enormous influence on our personality, work, and relationships with others.

Since money, or the lack of it, can have such tremendous influence, it is best to have financial planning. It is especially important to have financial planning if there is a known change of employment imminent. Such a change may mean a period of unemployment or less pay. It's always best to plan for the worst. That way you can realistically face such an adversity. If things turn out for the better, you can enjoy the benefits of the windfall.

We've all heard the saying "necessity is the mother of invention." In the case of financial planning, waiting until "necessity" dictates drastic action is too late to provide for flexibility in planning. In today's economy with its raging inflation, it doesn't take long for financial reserves to be exhausted. Once those reserves are exhausted and financial pressures begin to exert themselves, you are set up to be victimized. Employers are quick to sense desperate need on the part of the applicant and he will take advantage of your desperation. You will not be negotiating from a position of financial or emotional strength. Consequently, you may be hurt.

You may have planned every other aspect of your job search with care and commitment to finding an ideal job. If your lack of financial planning places you in a position of immediate necessity for funds, you may have to abandon your plan and take any job available. Therefore, it is essential that you include financial planning as an integral part of your plan.

How Much Is Enough?

You may be living a payday-to-payday existence now. If so, to provide for a financial cushion upon separation, you may now have to make budget cuts. Remember, unless you separate with a solid job offer or retirement pay, there will be no payday after you muster out.

If you have never budgeted family finances, now is a good time to start. Begin by listing your monthly commitments to:

- Housing/Rent
- Automobile (repairs, gas and oil)
- Food
- Utilities
- Clothing
- Education
- Insurance payments
- Entertainment
- Other time payments, credit cards, etc.

After you have compiled this list, multiply the sum by 15% and add that figure on as miscellaneous. There are typically other expenses but these are the most common.

To give you a good idea of what you may face, compare your current net income with this list to see how well you have been covering the expenses. Consider now the fact that the income figure changes to zero upon separation unless, of course, you will be receiving retirement pay.

To ensure a reasonable margin of security, you should have sufficient savings to cover these expenses for a two-to-six month period. If your savings are inadequate:

- Cut down on current expenses and save as much as possible

- Consolidate your payments into one that is manageable

- Prepare a lean post-separation budget

Perhaps the most important thing you can do is not plan for additional purchases of non-essentials. Get settled into a new job before you commit yourself to any additional expenditures.

It is surprising the naivete with which most separating military personnel face the civilian job market. One of the greatest oversights committed on their part is the competition they will encounter in the job market. The military person always has a job guaranteed while in the service. He competes within that service and his organization for a specific job, but a job and a paycheck, nevertheless, are guaranteed. It is not so in civilian life.

It may seem that with your skills and knowledge there are a number of opportunities awaiting you. Maybe so. But you still must compete against others needing and wanting that same job. You cannot blindly depend on the assumption that you are the person who will fill those specific demands. It is not only arrogance — it is foolishness.

Regardless of how confident you are that you can land a job upon separation, plan financially for a period of unemployment. That way you will be a winner in either situation. So how much is enough? Enough to carry you through a two-to-six month period with no pay check.

CONTINUE RESEARCH

By now you have conducted considerable research into your chosen job market and have started to prepare a target list of companies. At this time you could have possibly as many as three types of jobs you desire. Don't stop your research now.

Look at your choices in depth. Find out as much as you can about the city or cities you **may** live in. Begin by writing to the Chamber of Commerce of those cities requesting all information they can provide about their area.

Major realtors in those cities are an excellent source of housing information and prices. Write to the school districts, too, requesting information not only about schools and curriculum, but the costs, availability of transportation, and any other questions you may have.

Research any phase of target companies products, operations, and markets about which you can reasonably find information. Prepare lists of questions you will want to ask prospective employers concerning their company, products, or markets. Prioritize your choices. Once you are separated, you will want to be able to devote your time to contacting companies, not researching basics.

DECIDING ALTERNATE CHOICES

We don't always get exactly what we want. It is a common trait among people that they devote the majority of their time planning, plotting, and dreaming about their first choice in anything. Reality often is accepted only as a second or third choice. If we spent as much time planning for second or third best as we do first best, we might realize a far more acceptable alternative than fate deals out. Your future job is much too important to leave to the fickle fortunes of fate.

Alternate choices of job, company, geographic location, etc., will provide you with a sense of direction if the going gets tough on the job market. If you find yourself in the situation of needing a job because finances are running out, wouldn't it be nice to have already completed your research on your second and third choices? At such time you can implement your plan and feel confident you are not wasting your time at something that won't interest you.

It may have occurred to you to question if civilian job seekers are this thorough in their search techniques. Some are, to be sure; others may not be. Unless they are changing geographic location, industry, or job duties, they have an enormous advantage over you. They know:

- The city
- The industry
- Precise requirements of the job duties
- People in the industry

Also, they bring their reputation with them which is easy to verify.

People who are changing geographic location, industry, or job duties, will face the same disadvantages as you and they must compensate for it by research, training, and planning. Many of them will have gone through a civilian job search before and are "street wise" to marketing techniques. Essentially, they have learned the hard way -- by doing it and finding out what does and doesn't work.

THE RESUME

If you haven't done so already, now is the time to prepare your resume. Preparation of a good resume takes much time and thought. (See Chapter 7, THE RESUME.)

SUMMARY

During the period 9-5 months prior to separation you will be exposed to a lot of initial decision making regarding your future job. The difficult financial decisions will have to be made to enable you to be free of financial pressures while searching for a job.

By continuing research and planning you will gain invaluable knowledge of the industry in which you plan to work. You will have time to reflect upon your choices of geographic location, industry, and job duties. Deciding alternate choices will enable you to formulate plans in advance should you be forced to accept something less than first choice.

The resume, an important marketing tool during a job search, will be formalized and printed during this period. You're on your way to becoming an effective job searcher. Now you are ready to finalize your search plans and begin the execution phase.

ENCOURAGEMENT

You now have more knowledge of job research and planning techniques than do most civilians. By the time you separate, you will compete with the most seasoned job hunter.

PRE-SEPARATION

PLANNING AND RESEARCH CHART

Chapter 3 12-9 Months Prior	Chapter 4 9-5 Months Prior	Chapter 5 5-2 Months Prior	Chapter 6 2-0 Months Prior
Evaluation of Knowledge and Skills	Financial Planning	**Research Current Industry Literature**	Prepare Wardrobe
Define Job Duties	Continue Research	**Join Professional Societies**	Prepare "In Person" Contact List
Research Job Opportunities	Decide Alternate Choices	**Practice Interview Techniques**	Read Newspapers
Determine Your Market Factors from list below:	Prepare Resume	**Formulate Search Methods**	Contact Agencies
-Geographic Areas -Family Considerations -Demographics -Industry Preference -Company Size		**Begin Industry Contacts**	Study Your Chosen Professional/Skill Area
Research Sources of Information			Obtain Work Reference Letter from Superior

Chapter 5

5-2 MONTHS PRE-SEPARATION PLANNING

INTRODUCTION

It is during this period of time you will put the final touches on your plan and begin industry contacts. You still have some work to do in terms of preparing yourself for those all important interviews. The biggest restraint upon you at this time will be to move cautiously. Your availability to an employer is too far away at the 5-2 month period to waste your shots during this time. Remember, talk is cheap; commitment is real. That goes for both you and the employer.

Use the earlier months to plan your strategy, continue your research, and practice your interview techniques.

RESEARCH CURRENT INDUSTRY LITERATURE

Whether you plan to enter the job market in a skill area which is directly translatable from your military experience to civilian industry, or if you choose to enter a closely related or unrelated field, you should update your knowledge and skills. The quickest way to accomplish this is to research current industry literature.

It matters not if your chosen job is in a management role, a job in engineering, electronics, police science, food service, or whatever. There is current literature which contains valuable information on that choice. So, it's back to the library for research if you want to be well prepared.

If you are stationed at a remote location, a trip to a library can present a problem. One way you can gain access to the current literature is by asking for help from relatives or friends. Even strangers can help. When you want something in business, never be ashamed or too proud to ask for help. If you have a problem, ask for help. Need an answer? Ask for help. Americans are pushovers for the plea of help. When we hear a plea, we respond. When that plea makes sense, we react strongly. You will be absolutely amazed at the help you can get if you ask.

Write and tell that relative or friend what you're up to — and that you need help. They can send you select trade magazines, do basic, one time research for names and addresses of people in societies, companies, and agencies. That's not too much to ask and any information you can get will help.

As you should have already discovered, there are literally hundreds of trade magazines, publications, and directories in large libraries. Thoroughly read the latest issues of trade publications to learn what the latest innovations, technologies, and problems are in the industry of your choice.

For your chosen field of job duties, find out what the latest trends are in use of systems, equipment, or procedures. In sum, find out what is currently going on in your skill area or chosen industry. You may discover you are fairly well up-to-date with your knowledge and skills. Then again, if you are unaware of an obvious innovation, you may be embarrassed during an interview or on the job. Don't assume you know everything about your field. Don't even assume you know enough to acquire a job. No one has ever suffered from over-kill in job research. Many fall short in knowing what they are talking about. If you think you know it all, the challenge is clearly before you to attempt to disprove it by visiting your library. Chances are you will be humbled and be made a believer to the contrary.

JOIN PROFESSIONAL SOCIETIES

Professional societies are formed for the promotion of their profession and the mutual education, fellowship, and **help** of fellow members. Note the word "help." They have within their programs educational seminars, workshops, lectures, etc., on the latest systems, trends, policies and procedures within their areas of professional work. They welcome new membership. They, like most organizations, want to grow. A few will require some sort of professional certification before allowing you to join, but these are the exception. Most societies help their membership in gaining certification in their profession, if one is offered.

The information you can gain from joining a society, as well as the personal contacts you can make, will pay handsome dividends. In a recent case, a separated junior Army officer determined he wanted to work in the Material/Production Control profession. He knew precious little of the details of the profession but had a broad view of the work involved. He searched in vain for opportunities for a full five months. He then found out about the American Production and Inventory Control Society (APICS). After attending a meeting, he joined. Within 30 days, through the contacts he made in the society, he had four job interviews and was offered two positions, one of which he accepted. He is now training under a dynamic Materials Manager. What helped him get the job? His membership in a society and the contacts he made. His own enthusiasm and the interest he showed in learning all that he could about the profession convinced the employer that he was the person for them. The members of the society were ready and willing to help him.

PRACTICE INTERVIEW TECHNIQUES

You should begin to practice your interview skills. Chapter 8 is devoted to the discussion of the employment interview. You are probably your own best judge of your competence in, and knowledge of, interviewing techniques. In terms of landing a job, the employment interview is where it is "made" or "lost." The first interview, which may be your only one, is especially critical to your success. Therefore, as part of your planning and execution phase of your plan, digest the information on the employment interview well. You may want to read a book or two on interviewing techniques. The more knowledge you have on this procedure the better.

JOB SEARCH METHODOLOGIES

For the job searcher, there are really only four basic job search methodologies. They are:

- Resume distribution

- Referral contact

- Personal contact

- Agency assist

Let's discuss each of these methodologies so you can select the ones you want to use.

Resume Distribution

Resume distribution is the ultimate "fishing mission" job search method. It is, in reality, a direct mail campaign. Those people involved in direct mail campaigns for any reason should know what is traditionally the rate of return in positive leads. The percentage of return is in the 1 percent to 2 percent range. Not too encouraging is it? Then again, you must consider the value of the return. If you are selling a $16,000 item, one or two returns can pay handsome dividends if the mailing cost represents only a small portion of the profits before advertising. In the case of a job search, if the right response is received and a job offer eventually made, the time and expense was well invested.

Perhaps the biggest drawback to mass mailing of your resume is over-exposure in your particular marketplace. If you have mailed your resume to everyone and his brother and get no response, what's your follow-up position?

What resume distribution can do for you, if done properly, is expose your general qualifications to potential employers. The way it can harm you is that it can give a potential employer an incomplete picture of your qualifications devoid of any personality. The evaluation an employer makes on the content of a resume may preclude an interview until such time you are able to make a personal visit. If you never intended to visit the company in person, a direct mail campaign is one way of getting your qualifications there.

If you are going to mass mail your resume, don't make the mistake of trying to compose a general cover letter. Doing so only adds to the impersonal nature of the thing. Potential employers and employment agencies, both like to think they are the only ones receiving a resume. A general and obviously mass-produced cover letter will discourage them if they believe they are competing with hundreds of companies for your services. Take the time to write a short letter, addressing it, if possible, to the person whose name and title you found during your library research.

By not including a cover letter you leave so many factors of your availability in doubt, many people simply will not take the time to follow-up. Unless they have a critical need for exactly your qualifications, your resume ends up in the "round-file" instead of the small stack that's entitled "Arrange for Interview."

So if you're going to mass mail your resume, do it correctly. Take the time to write an individual cover letter. The information a cover letter should contain is discussed later in this chapter.

Referral Contact

Many service people have the advantage of dealing with suppliers, vendors, and other representatives of companies with which the military does business. Often these contacts can refer you to their employer or give you leads on companies they know employ people with your qualifications. In a job search, you are looking for information and leads. Ask for help.

Almost any job you have in the military requires you to use, operate, maintain, or service some kind of equipment. Therefore, you know about the equipment and have used it in connection with your job. Have you ever considered that the manufacturer or distributor of that equipment may be very interested in your knowledge? You just may be able to ferret out a contact and referral if you nose around a little.

Spread the word around to friends and relatives that you are, or will be, looking for a job. The folks back home generally hear about who is hiring and what type of skills are in demand. They probably have a very good idea of the industries in their city. Your friends who never joined the service may be able to give you a lead on a company or hiring official. You will never know if they can help until you ask.

Personal Contact

There is no search method that surpasses personal contact in attaining results. It is also the method which will require the hardest work and greatest patience.

Personal contact with employers is difficult while you're still on active duty. Some military people have used the provisions of terminal leave offered by some branches of service for this purpose. Chances are, though, that you will have to wait until you have separated to make the personal contacts you want, unless you're planning to stay in the city near your base or home port.

During personal contact with employers, you may encounter some frustrating and even irritating aspects of job search. Many companies, particularly the large ones, set aside only certain hours on certain days to accept employment applications. They will not even accept your resume or give you an application except during specific hours on those days set aside for this purpose.

Some receptionists and personnel clerks can be arrogant and impolite in civilian industry. Their sense of service is lacking the spirit and intent one finds in the military. There is no NCO sitting there overseeing the function to deliver the needed corrective action. You will find them inflexible for the greatest part. They, too, follow orders. Anyone's rank or position outside their company cuts little ice with them, especially if you're looking for a job. To alienate them will serve you no good purpose, even if you think they may have it coming. Be patient. Who knows, that person just may be reporting to you in a couple of weeks!

You never know what to expect during personal contact with companies. You may just fill out their application and leave your resume and be given the "don't call us, we'll call you" routine or, you may be ushered into the boss' office for an interview.

Personal contact is work. For the serious job hunter it should be a full day's work. To be effective, start at 8:00 a.m. and keep going until 11:00 or 11:30 a.m. Take a relaxing lunch break and then continue between 1:00 p.m. and 4:00 p.m. You will be tired and drained. You may be encouraged or you may be totally discouraged. Just don't give up. Stick to it. It's the steady rain that soaks.

All those personal contacts will bring results. As often as not, results come all at once. The cumulative results of all those contacts will seemingly "jell" within a very short period of time if you're on target with your particular skills.

There really is no way you can evade personal contact in job search. You can use the remaining search method to your advantage, but you probably have a lot to learn about it.

Agency Assist

You may want to use the agency assistance method of finding a job. Many people use various government and private agencies with shallow knowledge of their purpose and how they can, or cannot help. They are praised by some and cursed by others.

Understanding what the various agencies do and the way they operate will require an entire chapter to adequately address the subject. Chapter 13 is devoted to that subject.

BEGIN INDUSTRY CONTACTS

About 90 days before your separation you should start sending out resumes to target companies. Any time before that is too early for the vast majority of companies to seriously consider your employment. Sending a resume out earlier is risking that it gets lost or misplaced by the company because your availability is too far in the future.

By now, you have identified your primary target companies. Make every attempt to identify the individual, by name and title, to whom you want the cover letter addressed. The directories or other publications from which you have gleaned names and titles may or may not be correct. Most companies will understand the error if a change in that manager was made recently. It does, however, take away from the impact a correctly addressed letter makes.

You can be certain you are correct by simply telephoning that company and verifying the person's name and title. Don't tell the PBX operator you're looking for a job. Just say you want to write a letter to the individual who carries that title. If you say you're looking for a job, you will either get the personnel manager's name or be patched directly to that department. Don't give anyone the chance to tell you "we're not hiring anyone." They haven't seen your qualifications yet or even met you. For the right person, a job can be created. You just may be that person.

Address the letter to the person who you believe you would most likely work for or who will have the ultimate authority to hire you. If you cannot identify that person, address the cover letter to the Personnel Manager. Personnel departments like to think no one is hired except by or through them. But that is not always the case. It is often the case that someone other than Personnel is the hiring authority. It takes a very strong Personnel Manager with solid backing by top management to be in absolute control of hiring, particularly in the case of salaried personnel. Again, don't alienate the Personnel Department. If you're directed to go through them, you would be well advised to do so. They can be your greatest ally or your enemy. Why not make them an ally? If they are competent, your resume will receive proper distribution and evaluation.

THE COVER LETTER

In your cover letter state your interests. At this early stage of your search you can be quite specific in the type of job you're after. Tell them **why** you are interested in that type of job. Let them know when you are available for an interview and when you would be able to begin work. If you "fish-tail" on these dates, they may wonder just how serious you are about going to work for them or anyone else.

If you are going to be in their area, give them the dates and the local phone number by which they may contact you. No company is anxious to pay interview travel and lodging expenses. If they know you are going to be in the area, it will enhance the chances they will interview you.

Don't mention salary. What you want or expect in salary has no place in the cover letter. Keep your options on salary to yourself at this time. There is plenty of time later to negotiate. There may not even be the option to negotiate, but don't pre-judge the possibility. There are so many things to consider regarding salary that it would be foolish to even bring up the subject in a cover letter.

Keep the cover letter brief, informative, and to the point. If you're going to do any creative writing in the cover letter, you better know your facts and keep it relevant to what you're after. The employer is not seeking to be entertained nor does he want to spend a lot of time reading a letter from a stranger who may or may not fit into his organization. He simply wants someone who wants to work as the first criterion.

After forwarding your resume by cover letter to your primary target companies, do the same for companies of your second and even third choices if you have them. Restrict your mailings to secondary companies to about 25 percent of the number you mailed to primary companies unless your mailings are few. You want the best responses you can get. At this point in time you can afford to be choosy.

SUMMARY

By now you are getting an idea of how complex a well planned job search can be. The entire idea of a planned search is to give you a sense of direction. In order to be where you want, you must know how to get there. By identifying your skills and knowledge, you have accomplished the first and one of the most important aspects of a job search. Identifying the type job you want is next. Then you must know your market.

When these things have been identified, you should do everything you can to effectively present your qualifications to potential employers. This aspect of the job search is called "marketing" your skills and knowledge. What you are after at this point are employment interviews. Once you have the interview you can sell the whole you. Your skills, knowledge, and personality and the ability to project yourself all become important on that occasion. If you know the basic rules of job search, you enhance the odds of being hired. You're learning them fast.

ENCOURAGEMENT

You are not alone in your job search. People are ready to help. Ask them for it.

PRE-SEPARATION
PLANNING AND RESEARCH CHART

Chapter 3 12-9 Months Prior	Chapter 4 9-5 Months Prior	Chapter 5 5-2 Months Prior	**Chapter 6** **2-0 Months Prior**
Evaluation of Knowledge and Skills	Financial Planning	Research Current Industry Literature	**Prepare Wardrobe**
Define Job Duties	Continue Research	Join Professional Societies	**Prepare "In Person" Contact List**
Research Job Opportunities	Decide Alternate Choices	Practice Interview Techniques	**Read Newspapers**
Determine Your Market Factors from list below:	Prepare Resume	Formulate Search Methods	**Contact Agencies**
-Geographic Areas -Family Considerations -Demographics -Industry Preference -Company Size		Begin Industry Contacts	**Study Your Chosen Professional/Skill Area**
Research Sources of Information			**Obtain Work Reference Letter from Superior**

Chapter 6

2-0 MONTHS PRE-SEPARATION PLANNING

INTRODUCTION

During the final weeks before your discharge, the pace of activity will accelerate. The reality that you will be leaving the service and entering civilian life will begin to crystalize.

You also will be appreciative of any efforts you've already made in job search planning and research. You will be able to face the job market with a degree of knowledge and confidence experienced by few separating military persons.

The difficult decisions you've already made regarding the type of job you will look for, area you will live in, industry you want, etc., enables you to concentrate your efforts now within the framework of the search plan you have formulated.

If you will be working and living near your separating station, you can now start your personal contacts with prospective employers. If you are overseas or relocating, you will be restricted to correspondence or perhaps brief, initial job hunting trips while on leave or furlough. In any case, there is plenty of preparatory work yet to be done.

PREPARE WARDROBE

While in the military you became accustomed to wearing the appropriate uniform for the occasion. You were made aware of standards in grooming and dress. While there is a greater variety of styles and colors in wardrobe available to you in civilian life, there are dress codes in force. Violate a dress code in private business and the consequences can be embarrassing and harmful to your career. Fall short of acceptable grooming standards and you may find people talking about you behind your back. In short, people in private business have no more respect for the rebel against standards than do people in the military. In private business, people will let you hang yourself without a word of straightforward advice or counseling until the damage is done.

Your best approach to selecting your civilian wardrobe is to be conservative in your choices. Depending on the type of job you're looking for, don't over-dress or under-dress for the job. Two basic changes of wardrobe are sufficient in the beginning. That way, you have enough to appear at interviews in appropriate dress but have not committed your entire wardrobe choices before you get a feel for the way others dress in the company.

In many cases, regional differences in dress may require you to round out your wardrobe with quite different selections than your initial choices. The key is not to be "odd man out" in dress.

You should use your very best judgment in what you wear to an employment interview. At times, this decision is not easy to make. Some companies have a strict, written dress code. Most simply depend on their employees to dress properly and let peer pressure straighten out those who stray too far from norms.

Obviously, if you are applying for a job which requires manual labor in a dirty environment, you don't want to show up in a three piece Johnny Carson fashion label. Neat slacks, sport shirt, and some sort of jacket will do nicely. Then again, if you're applying for a job which will be in management or requires frequent contact with the public, a sport coat and tie is under-dressing. In any case, work on feeling comfortable in your new dress. Remember what the employer is looking for. He wants someone who is ready and willing to work.

Frequently you will see ads in professional publications and newspapers for "shirt sleeve managers." The connotation is that the manager is expected to dress as such but not let his dress get in the way of hard work. They want someone who will take off his suit coat, loosen his tie, roll up his sleeves, and work, even if it means helping a millwright solve a problem on a greasy piece of equipment. If you sit through the interview like you're worried your suit is going to get wrinkled or your suit coat isn't buttoned, you're not going to impress the employer.

Those who have been in the military for a long time may have had their social activities restricted to essentially military affairs. They may feel an inadequacy in selecting a proper wardrobe. Any large, reputable department store will have salespeople who know the up-to-date trends in styles. State your desires for a conservative business image and they can help you select appropriate colors and styles. Whatever you do, don't show up for an interview in a suit which clearly is out of style. Make the effort to be in tune with the times in terms of dress. It will save you embarrassment and enhance your chances of making a favorable impression.

For men, choices of dress in business are rather limited. The ladies enjoy a much wider variety of styles, materials, and colors. There are, however, most precise codes for styles of dress for certain positions. These choices vary among companies and the lady will be well advised to keep in step with those trends. Again, the salespeople in major department stores can help anyone with the appropriate choices.

PREPARE "IN PERSON" CONTACT LIST

For your first choices of employment prepare an in-person contact list. Even if you have sent a resume, plan to follow up with a personal visit. It is a rare occasion indeed when a company will hire a person based solely on the information contained in a resume. Even telephone interviews invariably must be followed-up with a personal interview.

The resume has so many shortcomings that personal contact is by far the best method of contacting prospective employers. You may have prepared a beautiful resume, but an employer has no idea of what you look like, your oral communications skills, or your personality. Photographs add little to the resume and probably do more harm than good. Why? The photograph is devoid of personality. You're permitting the employer to evaluate your basic qualifications and appearance without meeting you. That's too much to divulge without personal contact.

Don't be offended if the company lost or misplaced the resume you sent. Also, don't expect them to remember your name and background. You are probably one of hundreds who has sent them your resume in the past three months. Have another copy of the resume with you. Let them be embarrassed if they lost or misplaced it. It puts you on the offensive and them on the defensive. Don't make an issue of it. Just provide them another copy. No one is perfect and few Personnel offices are truly well organized.

During your personal contact with that employer, the object is to get an interview. In large companies where Personnel does all the screening, this can present a problem. They may well be in the position to choose whom they will interview and refer to the hiring authority. Don't let that discourage you. They can be persuaded to interview you. Through carefully selected and phrased words you can impress them with your desire to work for the company and that **not to be considered** for an interview would be very disappointing.

The statement "not to be considered" may strike a responsive chord. Employers must be very careful not to deny consideration in the broad application of equal opportunity laws. Don't use the phrase more than once. Either it will help you or go over their heads. If they are sharp, it will register. If it is mentioned in the proper context and tone, it may help you. They should not be antagonized if it is mentioned as a sincere desire for consideration, especially when no tone of threat is applied.

Most applicants will back off from a statement from Personnel that they have no openings or that they are not interviewing at this time. If you become demanding or abusive, your chances for an interview are nil. Instead, without begging or being "pushy," find out as much as you can. Show interest and enthusiasm; be to the point and polite. Ask for company literature. Inquire as to when they will be interviewing (not when they will be hiring).

If you have heard nothing from the company after two or three weeks, visit them again. Unless you were given clear instructions to phone for follow-up, go in person. It's so much easier to say "no" over the phone than in person. Don't give them the opportunity to do so. If the second visit doesn't pay off in interest, back off. Don't make a pest of yourself. Concentrate on your alternative choices and come back to them later.

Visiting only three or four companies does not constitute a job search. You have just begun. The idea is to visit as many companies as possible to acquire options. Don't **assume** a company doesn't have an opening or can't use you. A manager may be experiencing a real problem area in which he needs help and simply has not told anyone about it. The right person walks in and "presto" a job opening suddenly is created.

Because our society is highly mobile, people are changing jobs and moving from area to area as never before. This mobility creates job openings. In those industries experiencing growth, new positions are being created rapidly. There is a job out there for you, probably several of them. You can find them if you search properly.

READ THE NEWSPAPERS

It would be wise to subscribe to the major newspapers for the area in which you will be job searching. Many jobs are filled through help wanted ads. A large number of jobs advertised are not filled for a long time. This is because the "right" person simply did not apply. When you see a job that interests you, apply for it

Large public libraries subscribe to the newspapers for major cities. If you are conveniently located to one, you can save the subscription price by visiting your library on a weekly basis. Help wanted ads appear in the greatest abundance in the Sunday editions of newspapers.

CONTACT AGENCIES

There are numerous types of agencies which may be able to help you find a job. Many people use the various government and private agencies with shallow knowledge of their purpose and how they can, or cannot, help them. Understanding what the various agencies do and the way they operate will require an entire chapter to adequately address the subject. (See Chapter 13.)

STUDY YOUR CHOSEN PROFESSION/SKILL AREA

Continue studying your chosen profession or skill area. You must be prepared to hold your own in an interview situation where specifics of your knowledge will be tested. You can never know too much about your specialty. If you are targeting yourself for several areas of specialty, you should be well prepared in each of the areas.

WORK REFERENCES

At this time you should make arrangements with your superior(s) to obtain a letter of work reference. The prospective employer will appreciate your foresight in this matter since it is so difficult for them to check military work references. If you have had former civilian work experience, you should write to your former supervisor requesting that he furnish you with a work reference as well.

SUMMARY

Your personal appearance during an interview can have significant bearing on the impression you make on the interviewer. Negative hiring decisions can be made based purely on your appearance. Use good judgment in selecting your wardrobe.

As you begin your personal contact with companies, don't be upset if you encounter more inefficiency or indifference from what you're accustomed to in the military. In their own way, companies do get the job done. Be patient and politely persistent. Personal contact is hard work and can be discouraging. Newspapers are a good source for finding out about job openings although the majority of job openings are never advertised. Agencies can assist you in finding jobs. You should, however, be aware of their methods of operations. Continue researching details of your chosen profession or skill area. Stick with it. You will find a job.

ENCOURAGEMENT

You have a lot to offer business and industry with your skills. Presenting yourself properly is a key element in a successful job search.

Chapter 7

THE RESUME

INTRODUCTION

Resume writers, employment counselors, personnel managers, and virtually everyone else disagree on what format should be used and what information should or should not be included in a resume. Each view has supporters and detractors. It's difficult to find a concensus since each resume is, in itself, a creative document. What may be important to one person or situation, may not apply to the other.

The information contained in this chapter is based on working with thousands of candidates and client companies in a professional recruiting environment. The outlined format and content is one that is probably the most common in use throughout industry. Companies seem to prefer the format since it is easy to scan quickly and contains the salient information they need.

Before discussing the outline, there are some resume topics which should be discussed. They will help you to understand the purpose and uses of the resume and the information it contains.

PURPOSE OF THE RESUME

The **purpose** of the resume is to enable a candidate to present his qualifications, experience, and other essential data in capsule, written form. The intended **goal** in using a resume is to secure an employment interview with, or through, the organization receiving it. You can avoid many pitfalls and misconceptions by always remembering a resume's purpose and intended goal during preparation.

The resume should contain **facts.** The selection of which facts to include is the biggest problem for most people. It becomes a question of selecting those facts which you believe will be of most interest to prospective employers.

QUALITY OF THE RESUME

The quality of the resume can be judged from several perspectives, including:

- The content of the resume
- The organization of information
- The length of the resume
- The quality of paper on which it is printed
- The printing method

The resume should tell a lot about the person it represents. Not only does it contain basic facts about the person's education, experience, skills and knowledge, etc., but it can give you a clue to the type of person it represents.

The amount of care taken in preparing a resume varies widely. After an employer has read thousands of them and subsequently interviews their writers, he can make some value judgments based solely on the resume. These judgments can have considerable validity in terms of personality, imagination, and sometimes, professionalism.

One thing is certain. Each person who prepares a resume attempts to include only those things which will reflect favorably upon him. It contains the best possible portrayal of that individual by himself. While everyone understands that the resume contains the best portrayal of the person, not everyone believes that the information is complete or is thoroughly honest.

To be a complete resume in terms of information is not possible. There simply is not sufficient space in a resume to address other than the most basic facts. The statement that you possess a particular knowledge does not contain the qualification of how well you apply it or the depth of your knowledge. That type of information will be gleaned during the employment interview. The statement that you possess the knowledge may get you an interview but, upon examination, your depth of knowledge may be insufficient to the task to be performed and, therefore, will not qualify you for the job.

Terms like "complete knowledge," and "thorough understanding," are unwise to use in a resume. Even well known authorities in their areas of specialization would be careful in using such terms. Using them only invites the reader to question and challenge your knowledge or experience.

While modesty is difficult to find in resumes, honesty is a must. It is easy to inflate one's true qualifications in a resume. To support the inflated statement to a greater authority can be most embarrassing and damaging to your image.

Negative aspects of your life and work have no place in the resume but must never be denied if you are questioned about them. Should negative aspects of your life or work be addressed by the employer, admit mistakes but do not dwell on them. Everyone makes mistakes sometime in their lives. You will want to show a healthy respect for honesty by admitting failures, overcoming them, and accepting a lesson learned. Don't dwell on them! It may be that you disagree totally or in part with the factors or people that judged you in error or a failure in the past. Don't try the case anew with a prospective employer. Have in your mind brief, objective responses to such questions. Refrain from using invectives about people, or situations. Doing so will not help you. Change the subject by going on to your positive aspects.

Your resume can be a powerful ally in your job search if it is a quality document. It cannot make you something you are not. But different employers see different things in a candidate. With a quality resume you will enhance the chances that an employer will see something in you that he needs. Spend the time and money necessary to produce a quality product. It will help bring better results.

Content Of The Resume

A quality resume contains facts about a person and his collective knowledge, skills, and experiences which are relevant to the job for which he is applying. Complete relevance is difficult to attain but the relevant factors should be emphasized.

That is not to say a general emphasis resume cannot be utilized successfully. What you try to accomplish in a general emphasis resume is to cover all the bases with an incomplete plan. You leave it up to the other players in the game to figure out your direction and intentions. Only in the employment game, home plate comes in different forms than the singular description found in baseball. You must modify your plan (resume) to accommodate the intended goal.

If your sole purpose in preparing a resume is to find **any** job available for which you may qualify, a general emphasis resume is fine. Why settle, though, for something less than what really interests you and provides for fulfillment during your working years? Now is the time to plan properly for your chosen career path. A quality resume with the proper emphasis can help you attain your goals.

It is difficult to explain what is meant by the "tone" of the language used in a resume. A quality resume has a distinctive non-offensive, factual style. There is a universal distaste in a style which contains self-serving verbiage. A perfect example of this is the use of the individual's title or name in the body of the resume. Use of the name in phrases like "Mr. Jones was the recipient of the 'Engineer of the Year' award in 1976 by Hughes Aircraft," or, "Colonel Adams was the youngest person ever to be promoted to that rank," are in poor taste in the body of the resume. The person is identified in the first, or identification, section of the resume. Repeating the name in the body may do wonders for the writer's ego but it really has no place there. Outstanding accomplishments should be included in the resume but they should be stated factually and not combined with superfluous, ego-building language.

In an earlier chapter you were encouraged to use universal terms in explaining your duties and responsibilities. You were further encouraged to clearly identify your experience as being obtained in the military. The matter of identifying your experience as being in the military may be at odds with what others in employment counseling would advise. Judge for yourself what is proper, for you are the one who must support your facts. Be assured, though, that an employer does not appreciate subterfuge in a resume, however well intentioned. It is a fact you were in the military and it is sure to come out during an interview. Your military experience is very valuable to an employer. Learn how to sell it; don't hide it!

What civilians generally do not understand are all the acronyms used in the military. Organizational designations, likewise, are confusing and meaningless to them. You must use universal terms to identify and explain things. Done properly, the terms you use can create excitement and curiosity, providing you the perfect opportunity to expand on your experience. But don't let your answers lead to a general bull session about the military. Keep the conversation on a business level.

Equate military job titles to civilian counterparts. For example, you may have been NCO in charge of the Motor Pool. In civilian terms you will be more than likely a Supervisor, Operations and Maintenance of Motor Vehicles. If you list your military title, let the lead sentence of the description of duties clearly define the title in universal terms a civilian can understand.

You may want to modify the title to universal terms if it is clearly a military job title. If so, be prepared to support your claim to civilian job title. The key is to understand that you are essentially free to claim any title you want. The proof, though, is in your ability to demonstrate knowledge and experience supporting that title in the fullest sense from the civilian employer's understanding and perspective. That is probably the hardest job you face in marketing your military experience. That's why research by you prior to your separation is so important. Find out what's currently going on in the industry and discipline of your choice.

People in disciplines such as a machinist will have little trouble communicating with the civilian employer. On the other hand, a company grade officer of an Infantry unit is going to have a difficult time getting a civilian employer to understand his role because there are few **direct** analogies to cite. There are, however, many analogies you can cite in the application of leadership and organizational skills.

Depending on the job duties you intend to pursue, and the industry you choose, you can determine an appropriate title to try for **if** you know what's going on in that industry. That is where a universal title will serve you well in the resume. Titles such as "Executive" and "Manager" do have counterparts in military rank and title but should be used with discretion. In many cases it is wiser to use the military title of your job and then claim management responsibility in the lead sentence of the description of duties. Most civilians understand titles such as "Commanding Officer" and can glean analogies which apply to their business. You can honestly claim management or supervisory responsibility in the military, but that does not necessarily qualify you for the title "Manager" in a civilian business.

A former military person who served in a staff function can more safely claim the civilian title "Manager" and support it than can those in a line function. The reason is that most management line functions in civilian industry have the ingredient of P&L (Profit and Loss) responsibility. You will never convince a civilian employer you had P&L responsibility in the military. You can cite management of multi-million dollar budgets to no avail. The hard fact is that you did not have to generate one dollar in profit and that fact can be a shortcoming to claiming the title "Manager" in many civilian line management jobs.

You may be perfectly capable of assuming P&L responsibility and understanding the necessity for profit. You may be able to even surpass a civilian manager in your ability to attain them. But, the bottom line is that you are not a proven profit generator through management in their estimation. Although you may be academically familiar with the knowledge and skills required in P&L responsibility, until you have served in a P&L capacity you cannot claim the qualifications or the title of manager for many civilian industry line jobs.

There is no question that you had management or supervisory responsibility in the military and that fact should not be de-emphasized in the resume. Just don't expect civilians to understand that your responsibility can qualify you for a management position. They do not have sufficient understanding of the military just as you won't have sufficient understanding of civilian industry until you have had experience in it.

Therefore, when listing titles of jobs held on the resume, use good judgment. Universal titles connote the responsibility in civilian terms. Be sure you understand what the title connotes. It is often better to list the military title and then explain the management or supervisory responsibility in the lead sentence of the job responsibilities to preclude misunderstanding.

The content of a quality resume must give factual information. The true test of the content is in your ability to support the facts. An employer has to be burned only once by not verifying resume facts before he learns his lesson. As was stated before, you are free to make any claim on a resume. Just be sure you can support those claims. That goes for title, responsibility, education, skills and knowledge. Don't give reason for anyone to question your integrity. Proudly state the things that are meaningful and factual.

The content of the resume should be presented with good grammar and punctuation. Spelling must be without error. You are projecting an image of yourself in the style and care you exercise in preparing the resume. Give it your best effort. Have others read and critique it during the drafting stages. If you are not comfortable with the way it reads, re-do it as many times as necessary to please yourself, not others. You're the one who has to support its contents.

Professional resume writing services are available. Contract with one only if you feel completely inadequate to the task. You may walk out of the service proud as a peacock with the resume's style and content. But if your resume is professionally written, ask yourself the following questions:

- Is that really me?

- Can I support those facts?

If you can answer these questions in the affirmative, they have done you a service -- for a fee. In effect, all they have done for you is organize the facts. You had to provide the facts and explain them in universal terms. If you're not comfortable with the product, you have thrown your money down the drain.

Organization Of Information

The information in a resume should be organized and presented in a sequential manner which makes it easy for the reader to follow. There are several different formats you can choose from when selecting the manner in which the information is organized. Most libraries have books on resume writing and you may want to read them. You should select a style and format which pleases only you.

The most common organization of information found in resumes is as follows:

- Identification section
- Objective statement
- Academic credentials
- Work experience
- Personal data

There is nothing sacred about the format or the order of information. Other formats have features which provide for more data listing. Still others provide for a more essay type style and format which some people prefer.

What is most important is that the information flows in a sequence which will make sense to the reader. The above organization provides for the option of listing academic credentials before or after your work experience.

The rationale behind the positioning of one's academic credentials before or after work experience will vary with the person. Those with significant academic credentials seem to prefer listing them before their work experience. People with minimal academic credentials prefer to present their work experience first, followed by their education.

If an employer has in mind that a certain academic degree is required to fill a position, he may reject out of hand a very well qualified person who came up through the ranks or he may be persuaded by the experience listed that the person can do the job even if he lacks the academic credentials he originally considered essential. The choice is yours in which order you want to list academic credentials and experience. Your choice will depend on which qualification you want the employer to consider first.

Length Of The Resume

Keep the length of the resume to one page if it all possible. In no event should it exceed two pages. Those who include extensive details in their resume are risking that the reader will get bored.

In large companies where hundreds of resumes are received monthly, even weekly, lengthy resumes are an irritant to the staff. Apparently some resume writers believe that the longer the resume the better qualified the employer will think he is. The truth of the matter is that they will probably suspect the writer is overly impressed with his own qualifications or is unable to summarize his experience. For those people with extensive experience the best approach is to include only the most significant levels of responsibility in each job. Leave something to discuss during the interview.

Two or three letters of reference attached to the resume are appropriate if you have them. Attachment of military performance evaluations are of questionable benefit since the reader is not sufficiently familiar with them to judge their value. It is a good idea to have several of them with you when you have an interview so you can provide them if they are requested. Many employers will request a copy of your DD-214. Always have a copy of it with you when you interview.

Paper Quality

The paper used for a resume should be of good quality with a rag content of 10 to 20 percent. Paper itself does not the resume make. But, combined with its content, organization, length, and method of printing, it presents an overall image of the writer's professionalism. Don't scrimp on the quality of paper and don't go overboard either.

Don't use military stationery. Most military stationery is not standard business size. It is shorter in length and narrower in width. An employer can identify it as military stationery immediately. It just will not go over well to use it.

The choice of color of paper is a matter of individual preference. Some prefer a light buff color to white but it really makes no difference. A point to remember is that your resume may be copied for distribution to several people in the organization and the best copies are produced from white stock.

Stay with one or two sheets printed on one side only. Fancy "book" type resumes or one with multiple folds make them hard for the employer to work with and file.

Printing Method

A flawlessly typed individual copy of a resume is always in good taste. You will undoubtedly have need for multiple copies in your marketing effort. Selecting the method of reproduction is important if you want your resume to have a consistent appearance of quality.

The first class route is to have the resume typeset and printed on an offset printing press. Companies don't expect to see the resume typeset and it would add considerably to its cost. Offset printing, however, is the sure way of getting quality printing done. The quality control exercised in offset printing is far superior to any fast copy method. With quality rag content paper, the offset printing method will produce excellent copy and you will be proud of its appearance.

The fast copy machine industry has improved the quality of their copy tremendously in the past five years. Because they are limited in the type of paper you can use, offset printing at a print shop would be your best choice.

RESUME OUTLINE

You are free to choose any outline for resume preparation you desire. The outline discussed here is probably the most common format found in industry today. Each section discussion carries a corresponding letter designation for that section in the outline.

(A) The Identification Section

>This section simply identifies the candidate by name along with his street address, city, state, zip code, residence and business phone numbers.
>
>If you anticipate a move, it would be appropriate to include a contact address, phone number, and the date effective.
>
>Example:
>
>After November 3, 1981.   Address
> Phone number

(B) Objective Statement

>The way you can give yourself and the employer the most flexibility in the type job you will consider, and the job he will consider you for, is to state your objective in terms of development objective.
>
>Don't close the door to jobs of lower or higher level than your objective. Leave room for both of you to consider related jobs. Don't state your objective too precisely unless that is exactly what you're going to hold out for.
>
>Example of too precise an objective:
>
>"To be Purchasing Manager of a large company."

It is better to provide for opportunities related to Purchasing Manager with the objective of developing high level management skills.

Example:

"To develop high level management skills in Materials Management."

By wording your statement like this you open the door to many levels of supervision and management in warehousing, buying, inventory, purchasing, and Production Control. All of these disciplines have a career path leading to Materials Management. You haven't put yourself on record claiming a specific title or level of knowledge and competence. The employment interview will establish where and at what level you can assume responsibility. Your willingness to develop your skills is sure to interest the employer.

If you are "hung-up" on obtaining a management title in the beginning, you may reduce your opportunities. There is, however, a way to state the objective which implies you may accept only a management title but you're open to which level that will be.

Example:

"To continue development of my management skills in the Materials Management field."

There are subtle differences in stating your objective. These differences are extremely important in terms of flexibility. By being too general in your stated objective, there is a tendency to leave the employer guessing what interests you.

Example of a too general objective:

"To secure a management position which requires leadership and administrative abilities."

When you take the time to plan your search you direct your attention to those fields in which you feel qualified or wish to enter. You can then select the appropriate objective and select the facts for your resume which will support your objective. It may require preparation of more than one resume but the time and effort expended for a quality resume will produce the desired results.

(C) <u>Education</u>

Employers like to know the degrees conferred, name of your school, and the year the degree was conferred.

You may want to list the major and minor courses of study if they have significance from the general designation.

Example:

BSEE (Major in Semi-conductor Physics), University of Michigan, 1974

If your highest level of civilian education is a high school degree, simply list it as:

High School Graduate, 1974, Arvada, Colorado High School

You are wise to list military schools attended. List the military course title, an explanation in universal terms, and the duration of the course.

Example:

Machinist Mate "A" Operation of Steam Propulsion Systems 24 weeks, 1962

Your military training and education is valuable to a civilian employer. If the instruction you received in the military was in electronics, engineering, supply, administration, or whatever, list it. It counts!

High school and college level G.E.D. certificates should be included. Significant correspondence courses completed relating to your employment objective can also be listed to your advantage. There is virtually no separating military person who should have a lack of qualifications to list on a resume. If you think about what you have done and list it, there is plenty there to support resume facts.

(D) Work Experience

Starting with your latest job assignment, begin listing your work experience by inclusive dates the job was held. You can list either month and year for inclusive dates or years only if you have an extensive career.

Examples:

Oct. 78 - Present   _____

Jun. 76 - Sept. 78   _____

or,

'78 - Present   _____

'76 - '78   _____

Employers get very suspicious when significant periods of time are unaccounted for. The logical question is, "What was he doing during the nine month period not included?" They will either view it as a gross oversight or, suspect you're trying to hide something. Brig time maybe?

Given the nature of military assignments where temporary duty and other unique assignments are made, don't strain for complete accuracy on dates. Compute inclusive dates as closely as possibly so no blank periods are there. If you have to explain a temporary duty assignment, it is easier to do it in person during an interview.

Since space limits the information you can include on a resume, you may want to opt for summarizing earlier experience in one brief paragraph. For those retiring, you can cover the last 10 years or so in more detail and then list a 10 year period of inclusive dates with the earlier experience summarized.

Example:

1960-1970   Served in a wide variety of administrative positions of increasing responsibility including (titles or functions).

We have discussed military and universal titles of jobs in considerable detail already. You can list either your military title or a counterpart universal title. If the military title is unique without a universal counterpart, use the first sentence of duties and responsibilities to clarify the title.

Organizational designations are confusing to civilians. Use plain language designations even if they seem oversimplified to you.

Example:

You served in Headquarters, and Headquarters Squadron, 1st Marine Brigade. That will dazzle the civilian but won't tell him a thing. It would be better to say, "Administrative Unit" and let it go at that.

You can simplify things for the civilian's understanding. A Navy man would confuse the employer by listing his organization as CV-41, or SSBN 569. It will make far more sense to him by listing "Aircraft Carrier" or "Nuclear Submarine." Instead of confusion, you will generate curiosity about which ship it was you served on, if he's interested.

In an earlier chapter on the planning and research phase of job search you were encouraged to write a description of your current job as well as to make a listing of the responsibilities, skills, and knowledge you have accumulated while in the military. That data will now come in handy. Keeping your wording factual and brief, prepare a lead sentence describing your present job. In one or two subsequent sentences list other facts from the list. Equipment repaired or operated, technologies applied, and responsibilities are the type of facts you want to include.

In some cases it may be better to state the technology applied rather than the equipment worked on. In electronics, for example, the equipment is manufactured mostly by D.O.D. contractors but the technology is used by other companies. So, rather than listing equipment designations, state the technology.

Example:

Repaired and maintained digital circuit electronic equipment at the component level.

The above statement will open many doors as opposed to listing only one or two pieces of gear you worked on with which a civilian may not be familiar. If you received schooling and training in digital electronics, your basic knowledge can be applied in a wide variety of companies and on an even wider variety of equipment.

Sometimes the manufacturer's name of the equipment you worked on can be used to advantage if the manufacturer is well known in industry.

Use action verbs in describing your duties and responsibilities. You haven't been sitting on your hands in a passive state in the military. Get that message across to the employer.

Two or three sentences will usually be sufficient to describe your duties, responsibilities, and technologies applied for each of your previous jobs. If you have statistics to cite, make sure they are relevant and that they reinforce your level of responsibility. Too many statistics cited have a tendency to give the impression that you're impressed with your own self importance. There is a fine line between stating facts and "blowing your own horn" in a resume. Facts speak for themselves. Self-aggrandizement offends others.

The last sentence in the description of your job duties and responsibilities for each job ideally should contain a statement of the major accomplishment in that job. Employers, in fact, will often ask what was your greatest single accomplishment in your last job. The employer is looking for someone who will go the extra mile to make a contribution in his organization. Few people excel in every aspect of their job, but if they did not excel in some aspect, they were probably an average performer. Keep the statement factual.

(E) <u>Personal Data</u>

Personal data helps the employer get to know you. Keep it brief and divulge only the information you wish known.

<u>Marital Status</u>. Put married or single only. If you're divorced and single, put single. The employer may carry a prejudice against divorce. You may be divorced and have custody of dependent children. In that case, either leave your marital status off or list it as: single, number of dependent children and ages. Keep it honest, whatever you list.

<u>Health</u>. A statement of health is appropriate but it's up to you if you want to include it.

<u>Hobbies</u>. Sometimes the listing of hobbies will help. For those with limited experience, a hobby can give the employer a clue to his interests and job related skills. List too many hobbies and you risk the opinion that you don't have time to work.

<u>Relocation</u>. Your willingness to relocate can be very important to the employer. He may have just the job for you, but in another city or state.

SUMMARY

The purpose of the resume and the intended goal in using one should be kept in mind as you prepare it. If you talk to yourself in it and use it to support your ego, you're missing the mark. It is for the use of a prospective employer to evaluate and match your qualifications against his requirements.

Be factual and honest in the information you include. You must be prepared to support the facts when called upon to do so.

There are a number of styles and formats you can choose from when preparing your resume. The right one is the one you feel comfortable with. It is difficult to find agreement among employment counselors what information should be included in a resume. Each counselor's opinions will probably be based on their experience in industry. Each has valid ideas based on their experience. Select those recommendations which might suit your situation best and with which you feel comfortable. An outline of a resume follows.

ENCOURAGEMENT

You have valuable skills and knowledge needed in civilian industry. Take the time to present them properly in your resume. The resume will help you market those skills.

(A)   WILLIAM C. ADAMS
1644 Alder Avenue
San Diego, CA 97210

Home: (714) 420-2309
Work: (714) 437-5901

(B)   Objective: State your employment objective.

(C)   Education: Type degree, Institution name, year of degree

(D)   Work Experience:

        From - to date   Title, military organization, or civilian company name. One paragraph which includes: a lead statement of overall responsibility and authority; expanded statement of duties, skills, and knowledge used; and one sentence of the most significant accomplishment in the job.

        From - to date

        Etc.

(E)   Personal Data: Marital Status, Children(s) ages, Statement of Health, Hobbies, Willingness to relocate.

Chapter 8

<u>THE INTERVIEW</u>

<u>INTRODUCTION</u>

All your marketing efforts in job search are directed toward obtaining an employment interview. Your planning in job search should include preparing yourself for the interview.

The interview process is where **most** of the data used in a hiring decision is gathered by the employer. You never know when entering an interview situation what techniques will be used by the interviewer. They can throw questions at you which are designed to make you think on your feet. They will evaluate you and your qualifications based not only on the way you react to the question, but on the substance of your answer.

There are important preparatory steps you can take to be at your best performance level during an interview. Being aware of some interviewing techniques will help you respond properly. The tips given in this chapter for interview preparation will help you avoid some of the classical "boners" committed by job candidates. The interview can "make" or "break" you as a viable competitor. Be prepared.

SUCCESSFUL INTERVIEW TECHNIQUES

Accommodating The Employer

When you get a call to set up the interview, be as accommodating as you can. It isn't so much of a question of who needs who the most — you the employer, or the employer needing you; it is the beginning of your relationship with him. If you are hired, you will know who the boss is quick enough.

If you're the one who is in demand, be satisfied you're the one being courted. Starting the relationship with indifference or being difficult to accommodate will not serve in your best interests. Some employers can be very accommodating while others have neither the time nor the inclination to go through an elaborate mating ritual.

Should you have a prior commitment you cannot break, state so. Should an emergency occur after the interview time and date has been arranged, inform the company immediately. Then try to establish an alternate, mutually satisfactory time and date for the interview.

When distant travel is involved, most companies will make the arrangements and pay for transportation, lodging, and meals. Don't take for granted the tab will be paid by the company. If the employer isn't clear on the details, have him clarify them. Some companies will expect you to travel at your own expense and arrange for your own meals and lodging. Others will expect you to pay the expenses for later reimbursement upon completing their expense forms. Only you can decide if you want to pay your own expenses if required. How badly do you want the job?

Punctuality

Whether meeting plane schedules or driving across town, allow yourself ample time to be at the interview at the appointed time. It is impolite for either you or the employer to be late. Don't give him reason to doubt your reliability by being late.

If geographic considerations allow it, drive to the employer's place of business beforehand so you can easily locate it on the day of interview. Allow for travel time and such emergencies as flat tires or traffic jams. A safe way to do it is to plan to be in the vicinity of the employer's place of business one-half hour prior to interview time. Present yourself five to 10 minutes before the appointed time. If you get there earlier they may not be ready for you.

Grooming

Don't underestimate the importance of proper grooming. The grooming standards the military has are always in good taste in civilian life. One possible exception is the length of hair. More latitude on length of hair is usually given in civilian business and industry, but that does not give you license to do exactly as you please. They may not tell you to get a haircut; they simply won't hire or promote you if its a problem to them.

Some companies frown on beards. If you feel strongly about wearing one you probably would not be comfortable in such a company. Neatly trimmed beards or mustaches normally are not a problem, but don't be surprised if you run into an employer who expresses his dislike for them, particularly beards.

There is a sea of unwritten rules on grooming and dress in civilian business and industry. The best way to get a handle on them is through observation and your own sense of what's proper. Go out of your way to "do your own thing" in grooming and dress and probably no one will bother you. But you may have to pay a handsome price for that right in terms of employment and promotion opportunities.

Have your hair cut or styled and clean your finger nails. Check and double check your appearance as if you're preparing for inspection by the C.O. It may not appear obvious to you, but the employer will be inspecting and evaluating your appearance. A first impression is a lasting impression. Make it count.

Dress

During the planning phase of your search you should have anticipated proper attire for the job for which you will be applying. Inappropriate attire can cost you the job.

White Collar and Supervisory Jobs. If you have done any research about your market, the matter of attire will become obvious to you. The present day appropriate businessman's attire is an up-to-date, in season, three piece business suit. For the ladies, a women's business suit is your safest choice. The shirt or blouse should either be white or a light pastel. The accessories of tie, shoes, etc., should be in coordinated colors. The interview is not the place to test people's reactions to far out styling.

Public Contact Jobs. It is easier and safer to dress down to the working conditions once hired than be underdressed for an interview. Any job requiring public contact will demand up-to-date, conservative dress.

<u>Labor Jobs</u>. If you are applying for a job which requires heavy physical labor in a dirty environment, a suit would be inappropriate. A neat pair of slacks, shirt, and jacket will serve nicely. Use common sense.

The Employment Application

Most employers will ask you to fill out an employment application either before or after the interview. If so, don't get defensive and feel as though you're being singled out. Federal and state employment laws are such that an employer must at all times be prepared to defend or support a hiring decision for any one of numerous reasons. They are gathering data and simultaneously protecting themselves. A very high level candidate may successfully refuse to fill out the application, but that's pure arrogance. He is serving notice he will expect to be an exception to following rules. It is best to fill it out and not raise a fuss.

Fill out the application completely and don't leave blanks. If the item is not applicable, write "not applicable." Follow directions carefully and give complete information. Some employers are known to reject candidates based on their inability to follow directions on the application form. That may be an illegal practice but they do it anyway. When there are hundreds of applicants, seemingly insignificant factors can be used to sort out the excess.

Use your best penmanship and grammar. Be completely honest in everything you write. Usually the application calls for references. To be properly prepared, you should have a list already prepared so that you can list them quickly. Names, addresses, and phone numbers of three or four references should always be carried with you when job hunting. The employer is primarily interested in work references, not in personal references. He will appreciate a copy of a reference letter from your last military superior and any other written work reference.

Don't take all day in filling out the application. Someone is waiting to interview you.

If there is a question asking what salary you want or will accept, write "open." The employer may ask you why you wrote "open." Tell him you didn't have complete information on the duties and responsibilities of the job and that you consider that information, along with the type of benefits the company provides, important to your idea of what the job should pay.

You should not commit to any salary until you have **all** the information you want about the job and benefits. When the salary is negotiable, you don't want to commit yourself prematurely. Chapter 9 is devoted to the discussion of salary and negotiation. You are encouraged to study it well.

The Hand Shake

During your introduction to the employer, smile, give a firm handshake, and tell him you are pleased to meet him. Speak up and don't mumble your words. Look him straight in the eye.

The handshake is more important than you may think. A limp handshake either goes unnoticed or registers as a lack of confidence in yourself. If you have a very strong grip, don't make it a test of strength. The unfortunate interviewer may suffer from rheumatism, in which case you could actually hurt him. That would not enhance your chances of gaining employment.

Smoking During Interview

Generally, it is best not to smoke during an interview. Smoking is not a graceful act and it is very offensive to many people. In recent years there has been a revolution of sorts by non-smokers to exercise their right to breathe fresh air. Don't risk offending the interviewer.

In the past, it has been an accepted interview technique to offer the interviewee a cigarette to place him at ease and establish rapport. If that practice has not been changed, it should be. The concept is still valid but the vehicle for accomplishing it should be re-evaluated.

If the employer smokes and the interview drags on to a half day or longer, it's all right to smoke. By that time he is probably feeling uncomfortable that he is offending you.

Use your best judgment on the matter of smoking during the interview. Your abstinence will do your health good and you won't risk offending the employer.

Martini Lunches

You may be invited to luncheon or dinner by the employer. Again, use your best judgment. Never order more drinks than your host. Drink only what you can **absolutely** handle without affecting your speech, gait, and thinking ability. Know when to quit and switch to coffee. One or two drinks should be sufficient to establish sociability. You don't have to compete with the host on the number of drinks consumed. The fellow, or lady, may have the proverbial "hollow leg" and drink you under the table.

If you are a teetotaler -- stick to your guns. Very few jobs require that you be a drinker; stay away from those that do. The employer may imply that drinking is a prerequisite for the job if a lot of entertaining is required. Without getting defensive about it, tell him you're comfortable entertaining both those who do and do not drink. If that doesn't satisfy him you probably won't be comfortable working for him.

Some employers are known to ply the applicant with drinks to see how far he will go and how well he can handle such a situation. You may end up having a great evening from your perspective, but you probably won't get the job offer if you drank to excess.

Eye Contact

Maintain eye contact with the interviewer. For some people this is very difficult to do. In order to avoid doing this, they naturally fix their gaze on an inanimate object when formulating thoughts. Others become shy or lose confidence in an unfamiliar or stressful situation. If need be, discipline yourself to maintain eye contact. It is very important during an interview.

Eye contact is a powerful use of body language. Everyone has experienced it at one time or the other. Just get someone angry at you and you can appreciate the influence eye expressions can have. Both you and the interviewer will be watching for signals of reaction through eye expression. Through eye contact, each of you can catch expressions of approval or disapproval in your responses to questions. The interviewer doesn't like to be robbed of those expressions and you shouldn't be either.

Suffice it to say that if you apply for a supervisory, management, or sales position and don't maintain good eye contact, you probably have forfeited the job.

Listening And Talking

It is better to be a good listener than a talker during an employment interview. Some employers will give clear expressions of what they are looking for in talent and personality during the interview. You can pick up on these clues and respond accordingly.

Let the employer talk all he wants. If he gives you his life's history or tells you of his success, listen attentively and with interest. He is probably trying to tell you something in terms of what he is looking for. Some employers are poor interviewers and only know how to talk about themselves.

One of the greatest shortcomings by job candidates in listening ability is that they hear what they want to hear, not what is being said. Listen very carefully when things like job responsibility, promotion opportunities, and pay raises are being discussed. Now is the time to prevent later misunderstandings in such matters.

Evaluate the opportunity realistically, for in the future if promotions or raises are not forthcoming at the time you **thought** they would be, one of the following conditions is probably evident:

- Your performance is not at a level to support a raise or promotion;

- The employer is not following through on what he said; or

• YOU WEREN'T LISTENING WELL

Assumptions are things we often operate on to our later disappointment. Rosy pictures can be painted with words which are written with disappearing ink. You must evaluate implied promises carefully.

Almost every employer will give the candidate a positive view of the job, work conditions, and opportunity for upward mobility. By asking questions you can probe into the details of these factors. If you don't press too hard or too long on the issue you can usually uncover the realities. When the employer outlines hard work, problem areas, or no promotion opportunities, believe him. Don't rationalize the situation into something that doesn't exist.

Answering Questions

When questions are asked of you, give brief, factual answers. Keep your responses positive in nature. If negatives are thrown at you, give a positive response. For example, the employer may tell you that you will be required to work involuntary overtime and Saturdays when necessary. The proper response is that you've worked long hours and on weekends before.

It may be that those features are a very negative aspect of employment to you. Just don't give a negative response. File the information in your mind for consideration if the job is offered. Give a negative response or signal and you may never be offered the job. Remember, what you're after are job offers, options from which you can choose. It may be that this particular job is the only one offered to you. It is far better to work overtime and Saturdays than to be unemployed.

It is gratifying to receive a job offer, even if it's not the job you really want. It is ego-shattering to be told you were not qualified or not the one selected for the job. It will be a rare happening indeed when you get a job that is satisfactory in all respects. If you have options to select from, you can make the trade-offs you feel you want to make and select what you believe will be the best opportunity.

Be decisive in your answers to questions. If the employer is a sharp interviewer, he will throw questions at you that will require you to evaluate a situation and give your recommended solution. Don't hedge on your answer. Give your decision and the thinking or reasoning behind it. Sometimes the question will not have a "best" response. If you try to outguess what the employer is thinking and give an answer that you believe will please him, you're not being honest with yourself. What the employer is doing is testing your knowledge or decision making ability, or possibly both. You want the job and you believe you're qualified to do it. Convince him of it. If you can't convince him, you won't get the job.

Asking Questions

After the employer has asked all the questions he wanted answered and has given you the information he had to give, it's your turn to ask questions. Get excited about the job. Ask questions not only about the job you're applying for but about the organization overall. Questions like how long the company has been in business, its sales volume in units and dollars, peculiarities of their market, etc., will show that you have a broader perspective and interest than what the job you have applied for encompasses. Your past research will pay-off at times like this.

Ask the employer about employee turnover. Find out if the employees are unionized and how good the company's relationship is with the union. Clear-up any other questions you may have about the job content and then, **ASK FOR THE JOB.** By expressing a desire for the job, you tell the company that you want to work for them.

Your mission in an interview is to make that employer want you so badly that he is ready to hire you at the best salary he can offer. Your enthusiasm, interest, and responses to his questions are important to that choice. Your background may not be exactly what he is looking for but you should have convinced him you can do the job.

Salary Negotiations

There is an important aspect of the job interview that still must be covered. That is the matter of salary and benefits. Salary and benefits are usually the last topics covered in an interview. You don't have to tell the employer that salary is important to you. He knows that already. Don't rush the issue. Let the employer be the first one to mention salary. The employer is not anxious to pay anybody any salary. His greatest concern is finding the right person with the best qualifications. He probably feels anybody would be glad to work for him and his company and that the salaries he pays are outrageously high. He is entitled to his opinion.

What you want to do is make him believe that your work means everything to you. Once you have established that type of belief in him, then, and only then, are you ready to start talking salary. His idea of proper salary for the duties and responsibilities of the job may not match yours. They seldom do. But you have established the most fertile ground for harvesting the best salary possible.

For higher level jobs, salary and benefit discussions may not take place until the second or third interview. The employer may be very flexible on salary depending on the individual and his qualifications. Don't rush the issue. Its turn will come when it is appropriate for the employer.

FOLLOW-UP

After the interview, follow up with a letter expressing interest in the job. Thank the employer for his time and courtesies extended.

The simple act of a follow-up letter is impressive. It is surprising how few job candidates use this device to keep the lines of communication open. Virtually every job has as part of its duties some sort of follow-up action required. Your follow-up with the employer immediately establishes your ability and awareness for follow-up. It will set you apart from your competitors.

If a second interview is scheduled, you know you're in serious contention for the job. Make the interview on the appointed time and date. You may want to have in mind several in-depth questions about the job which will re-establish your interest in it. Go for it!

WHEN THE OFFER IS MADE

At such time the offer is made, clear up any questions you may have about the job, salary and benefits.

The employer will usually indicate when he wants your decision. If he pushes for immediate acceptance, do so only if you feel sure you understand everything and are ready to go to work for him. A few days to a week is ample time to consider any job offer. Only those people who are in great demand can afford to bask in the ego trip of considering a job offer for an extended period.

Employers do not like to hear that you may be waiting for another offer. That puts them in the position of thinking that they may be second best in your mind. If you are considering another offer already made, then it's all right to mention it. Who knows, he may up the ante? But don't play games. State it as a fact and the employer will evaluate the situation for himself. Again, it is only those in great demand who can afford to pit one employer against another competing in salary.

You may miss the opportunity if you're waiting to receive another offer. What do you have left as possibilities if you turn down this job and the other offer does not come through? This offer will give you an excuse to contact the one you're waiting on. Unless you're in demand though, be prepared to be told to go ahead and accept the other offer because they just have not made a decision. It's a calculated risk you take but one which will bring the matter to a head. Don't keep the employer who has made you the offer waiting too long. He is entitled to a timely response.

SUMMARY

The employment interview is an exciting and stressful situation. It is where the employer gets to evaluate your personality, experience, and background. It is a common occurrence to hear candidates say after the fact, "I wish I would have ...," or, "If only I had thought of ..." The chances of you responding and reacting exactly right to every interview situation are negligible. The very fact that you are unfamiliar with the interviewer, his experience and values, gives potential for unlimited "improper" responses from his perspective. You must trust that the interviewer has a balanced perspective in evaluating the responses you give.

You can anticipate questions which will be asked and have responses formulated in your mind. Any amount of preparation you do will be better than no preparation. Following the basic rules of good dress and grooming, listening, and conduct during the interview will focus the employer's attention on those positive aspects of you and your experience that count. Good manners are always in style. They are especially important to you during an employment interview. Be warm and friendly but always maintain a business-like attitude. In all things, show the same respect for the employer that you would want if you were in his shoes. You have his interest in you as a potential employee. Keep that interest alive.

ENCOURAGEMENT

You have learned to interact with more people of diverse backgrounds than most civilians do in their entire lifetime. This fact will serve you well in adjusting to different personalities during employment interviews.

Chapter 9

SALARY AND BENEFITS

INTRODUCTION

One of the most difficult tasks facing you during the transition from military service to civilian employment is the evaluation of your worth to an employer. The irony of the situation is that what you think you are worth is not as important as what a **given** employer thinks you're worth.

Millions of your predecessors have helped establish the value of former military experience in hundreds of disciplines in a wide range of businesses and industry. There is no concrete data available to help us identify this worth. Therein lies the dilemma.

The best way you can view the situation is from the perspective of the supply and demand for your skills, knowledge, and experience. Research of your job market can help you determine existing levels of worth (compensation). Your greatest task will be in relating where you can realistically fit into the scheme of compensation levels. The following discussions will be helpful in determining this.

PRECONCEIVED WORTH

It would be a mistake to target yourself to a preconceived dollar amount in salary. There are so many variables to take into consideration when job searching that to limit your search to accommodate a preconceived salary level is unwise. By listing some of the variables, you can begin to appreciate the necessity of keeping the salary "open." Among the most important are:

- Your own marketability
- Geographic area in which you plan to work
- State of both Federal and local economies
- Supply and demand
- Size of company
- Viability of the company
- Level of your entry into company
- Responsibility in the job
- Pay of others in the company
- Travel involvement
- Hours of work
- Benefits offered
- Range of salary within job
- Opportunity for upward mobility

These and a score of other variables will influence the salary level of a given job. By establishing a preconceived salary level you could be disqualifying yourself from many jobs which offer attractive benefits, upward mobility, or other desirable features.

SALARY COMPARABILITY

Unless you plan to work in Federal Civil Service, you should not try to equate too closely your present job and rank to civilian industry salaries. Civilian salary comparability is a highly publicized concept which defies application. If you attempt to do so you will be comparing apples with oranges. It is true that military people are underpaid for their skills, responsibilities, and hours that they put in and should be raised to the levels of comparable salaries of those performing similar skills and having similar levels of responsibility in civilian industry. But to say one can step from one environment to the other with full comparability in salary simply is not possible in most cases.

Even in the most technical of specialties, electronics for example, full comparability is hard to justify if you're talking about shifting the people between military service and civilian industry. Why? People in military electronics maintain and operate the equipment, they do not manufacture it. If they find a job operating and maintaining similar equipment, then comparability is applicable. If they are going to work in manufacturing, however, they will require some training and orientation to acquire a comparable level of expertise in manufacturing operations.

Many civilian organizations will not take the time or spend the necessary money to enable the ex-military person to make the transition. Because of their shortsightedness, they are the losers. That's when your ability to sell your skills and knowledge can best be utilized in job search.

The ex-military people who can find work doing the same thing they did while on active duty, with the same equipment or systems, can hold out for comparability. But they must ensure it is **fully** compatible with only slight variations. In these cases, their experience is probably superior to civilians and they should have no trouble.

Now let's consider a reversed situation. What would your reaction be if you were in charge of a military unit where a civilian was given a fairly high rank and assigned to your unit because he had comparable skills, but really knew little of your organization, procedures, peculiarities of assigned equipment, or mission? If you had a choice, would you take a slightly less qualified military man of lesser rank, or the civilian? You may howl, "unfair analogy!" Not so. You're as much of an unknown risk to that civilian employer as the civilian would be to you. Remember, the employer is living and working in as much of a closed society as you in terms of exposure to other industries. Chances are he has a choice to exercise. If so, he will select the person who can do the job best. If you're that person, you will have to convince him of that fact during an interview.

You're not being encouraged to seek a job at a lower level than your expectations. Just don't tack a title or salary level to it. If you commit yourself to title or salary level, you're feeding your ego and also doing yourself a disservice. Simultaneously, you may be lining yourself up for disappointment and perceived dissatisfaction because you didn't get what you wanted. Keep your options open and flexible. This doesn't mean you have to accept the job, but what you do find may be the best available at that time.

YOUR MARKETABILITY

Generally speaking, as an ex-military person your marketability is very good. In other words, your skills and knowledge are in demand. The secret lies in your ability to market yourself and your skills and knowledge.

In many cases, your skills and knowledge will be a perfect fit and your military experience will be viewed as a plus by the employer. It's in those cases where your skills and knowledge are not a perfect fit that problems may arise. Many employers will not have an understanding of, or appreciation for, your capabilities. It is in these types of situations that you must be able to draw on analogies which apply to the job you're seeking.

If you have a military specialty which is so unique that there are few civilian counterparts, your marketability is reduced. If you want a complete change in job duties from those you performed in the military, your marketability may be reduced because there will be few analogies to draw on. Civilians switching career paths face the same reduction in marketability. But this doesn't necessarily mean there are no opportunities. It means, simply, that your marketability for certain jobs has been reduced. Consequently, you may have a tougher time convincing the employer your background is suitable for the particular job for which you have applied.

It is a fact that a person's marketability is reduced when he is unemployed. As a separating military person, you have the best reason for job change and a short period of unemployment. Unfortunately, though, you will fall into the general category of "unemployed." Employers like to hire people who are already employed. When one has been in the employment function for a number of years, a pattern emerges that places a general suspicion on the reliability of the unemployed.

As a recently separated military person with an honorable discharge, you will largely escape the reduction in marketability because of unemployed status that others experience. However, your negotiating position is weakened as it is for any other person currently unemployed. This should tell you something to consider in the future: Don't leave one job until you have another secured.

THE ART OF NEGOTIATION

The art of negotiation involves discussion and settlement of terms. Ideally, everyone gives a little and gains a little. The ultimate agreement should be satisfactory to all parties. Salary negotiations should not take place in an atmosphere of adversary role and confrontation as is the case of management and labor union negotiations. A gentlemanly, businesslike atmosphere will produce the best results. There should be no hard feelings by either party once the terms have been settled and no one should feel they were taken advantage of. Negotiations should be viewed as a due course business transaction — no more, no less.

In salary discussions, supply and demand of the candidate's skills, experience, and knowledge, have tremendous bearing on his position of strength in the negotiating process. Separating military people have trouble evaluating their position of strength because they lack knowledge of, and experience in, the civilian marketplace. Too many of them enter salary negotiations with the general feeling that they were underpaid in the military or that they should receive a salary at an equivalent level or more. These factors alone have no bearing on your worth to an employer. What really counts is the degree of need he has and how closely you can fill his requirements.

For salary negotiation purposes, your lack of knowledge and experience in the marketplace can be offset by research. When you target yourself for certain types of jobs, you should endeavor to find out what are reasonable salary ranges for the jobs in the particular geographical area. The unsophisticated job searcher sets a salary level in his mind, applies for jobs in different disciplines and industries, and then wonders why he has such trouble finding suitable opportunities. Don't fall into this trap. Identify your strengths and your market. The salary will fall into place.

The first rule of salary negotiations is this: Evaluate both your and the employer's position of strength. Obviously, if you enter negotiations with a one-sided evaluation, you probably are headed for trouble. While no one should **feel** they were taken advantage of in negotiations, that doesn't mean one of the parties will not take advantage of the other if they can. Lack of knowledge of what you're negotiating or lack of negotiating skills puts you at a disadvantage if the other person is well informed. To be sufficiently prepared for salary negotiations, you should know:

- Your strengths
- Your market (supply and demand)
- Reasonable salary levels
- Negotiating skills

CONDITIONS FOR NEGOTIATION

Not all employers give the candidate an opportunity to negotiate salary. There is an element of judgment that must be exercised to determine if negotiations are appropriate. You may encounter any one of the following approaches to salary offers and negotiation:

- A firm statement of fixed salary
- A statement of salary offer
- A request for your statement of salary desired, or
- A statement of salary range

There are employers who have a tight budget and have established a fixed salary for the job regardless of the qualifications of the applicant. They leave little room for negotiation by giving a firm statement of fixed salary. They state the salary and follow the statement with the comment, "That's it; that's what the job pays," or, "That's it, that's what the job is worth."

You will take a calculated risk by trying to negotiate a higher salary. The employer is probably trying to tell you the salary is not negotiable and for you to either take it or leave it. Unless the salary is very close to your bottom line, you may have no choice but to turn it down. If you plan to decline the job even if he doesn't raise the salary offer, you might be able to state your requirement and get it. Under conditions like this, an equally blunt statement may get results. You may want to try something like, "I want the job, make it (your desired salary) and you'll have yourself a darn good employee." Unless your dollar figure is very close to his offer, you probably won't stand much of a chance of getting the job.

Other employers will make a statement of salary offer. They will leave the door open to negotiation by omitting a firm statement of fixed salary. In this case you must judge for yourself if the right conditions exist for negotiation. Knowing your market will help you make that determination. If the salary sounds fair to you, you're not obligated to negotiate. But, there are other things to consider besides the basic salary. What does the job entail? What are the benefits? What are the working conditions?

If you have determined the salary is too low for the duties and responsibilities outlined but you really would like to have the job, you should attempt to negotiate. Begin by telling the employer you want the job but that the salary strikes you as being low for keeping a person in the job. Tell him, "If that's the most you can pay, I understand. But the job is so (good) (interesting) that for the right salary I would take it in a minute." If he is open to negotiation, you're on your way in the discussion. Otherwise, he will slam the door on negotiating and you will be back to the "take it or leave it" situation.

An employer who is prepared to negotiate salary from the beginning will either ask you what salary you're looking for or will give you the salary range for the job. If he does either, the conditions will be right for negotiation.

EXCHANGE INFORMATION

When an employer begins salary negotiations with a question like, "What level of salary are you looking for?," weigh your answer carefully. Curt answers like, "The most I can get," or, "Enough to live on," will eliminate any chance you had to intelligently pursue negotiations.

If you propose a salary before you even know what the range is, you could be committing a serious blunder. You might overshoot his range to the point that he feels negotiating further would serve no useful purpose. Even if he were successful in negotiating the salary downward to his range, how happy of an employee would he have? Even worse, you may quote such a low salary that he immediately accepts. Later you may find that others are paid more than you for performing the very same tasks or that he was prepared to pay you much more. In either case, it would be your lack of negotiating skills that brought on the problem.

Another thing you wouldn't want to do is to ask him simply, "What does the job pay?" You may not like the answer.

What you should do is throw the ball back into his court. To do this, ask him what the salary **range** is for the job. Note the word "range." Have the employer commit to a range so you know your negotiating parameters.

If you have not previously established what the benefits are for the job, now is the perfect time to ask for details and clarification. The benefit package may have significant influence on your idea of what a good salary range should be. Remember, benefits may be considered tax-free income from the perspective of an employee.

Once you have established the range and the accompanying benefits, the ball has been returned to your court for a decision. It is **always** a difficult decision. You don't know what the employer is thinking and you want the best salary he is willing to pay. If you have been a good listener, he may have given you a clue as to what he is willing to pay. When he gave you the range, did he associate education or experience desired or required for different levels? If not, ask him for some representative guidelines. You're not a mind reader and he has all the information you need for an intelligent decision. Dig it out of him politely! Once you have the needed information, evaluate it quickly against your qualifications, and state the **range** you would accept. Again, notice, **the range.** Make the low end of your range what you will accept with the upper range as a nice option if he goes for it. Keep your range narrow but provide him the option. Now the ball is back in his court.

If he quoted a range that is considerably below what you believe is a fair salary for the duties and responsibilities outlined, you must be prepared to attack the problem from another angle: Your services are worth more; the job is not under-salaried. Rarely will you find an employer admitting that the salary is too low for the job. The exact same position in another company may pay more or less. That isn't the issue. Maybe that's all this employer can afford to pay. In this case both your negotiating and your selling skills will be tested.

You will probably have to indicate that the top of his range is lower than you would accept. At this point it probably would be best to state your bottom line figure and let the chips fall where they may.

If your bottom line figure is within his capability, he should now come back with a firm offer. If this offer is in your range, you can either accept on the spot or request time to consider it. Do not accept on the spot unless you understand the total salary and benefit package.

If his offer is below the range he quoted for the job, you have some serious thinking to do. He may have made a low offer because, for some reason, he does not believe you are sufficiently qualified to be within the salary range for the job and if you accept the offer, you may have a real uphill battle to prove yourself. Is it worth it?

LETTER OFFERS

At times employers extend offers by letter. Once the offer is made by letter, your opportunity for negotiating salary is very limited. It is best to have the negotiations completed before you leave the interview.

SALARY LANGUAGE

Make certain you and the employer are talking the same language when salary figures are quoted. The following classical case will illustrate how an agreement was reached on salary, and how the use of different languages led to a colossal misunderstanding.

The employer asked the candidate what he was looking for in salary. The candidate said, "Nineteen." The employer agreed and the deal was struck. When payday came at the end of the month the employee's gross pay was $1,583.33, which equates to $19,000 per year. The irate employee thought the employer had agreed to $1,900.00 per month, or $22,800 per year! Their relationship ended that day. Both parties learned a lesson.

BENEFITS

A benefit is something of value or a service which is available to the employee beyond his basic salary. At executive levels, they are called perquisites, or "perks." Just to give you an idea of the wide range of benefits used in civilian business and industry, here is a partial list:

- Profit Sharing
- Bonuses
- Stock gifts
- Stock options
- Stock Purchase Plan
- Buy and Sell Agreements
- Homes
- Housing allowances

- Cars
- Car allowances
- Expense Accounts
- Use of vacation facilities
- Insurance (including medical, life, optical, dental, prescription drug costs, disability)
- Paid Relocation
- Temporary Lodging
- Help in obtaining mortgages
- Reimbursement for some home purchase expenses
- Vacation pay
- Holiday pay
- Retirement Plans
- Travel expenses
- Membership in Clubs
- Cafeterias
- Tuition Aid
- Children's Education Expenses

To consider such a list of benefits is stupefying. What are their worth? What can you reasonably expect? First of all, some of these benefits are offered or negotiated only at the highest executive levels. Just as flag rank in the military has certain perquisites, executives in civilian industry enjoy extraordinary "perks."

Outside of the benefits negotiated as part of union contracts, benefits are dispensed at the pleasure of the owners of the company. Benefit packages run the entire spectrum from outstanding to none. It all depends on the company. It has become increasingly necessary for companies to become competitive in benefits to attract and retain employees. Some companies, though, somehow seem to survive while offering very limited benefit packages.

Some companies simply cannot afford to pay for good benefits. The salary and benefit dollars paid to employees are the biggest operating expenses for almost every company. If their profit margins are slim because of competition in the marketplace, the benefit package suffers.

Most companies have their benefit packages formalized and will not vary from the provisions except for the highest levels of management. It would be a serious mistake on your part to attempt negotiation of benefits if the company's program is formalized, already liberal, and if the job you are being considered for is not in management. In most large companies, management has built-in perquisites in the benefit program and you will want to evaluate carefully if it would be reasonable to attempt negotiation for additional perks.

It is more important to understand the provisions of an existing benefit program than it is to worry about having to negotiate items. All is not what it seems, or what you may have heard, concerning the benefits civilian employees enjoy. Let's dissect and examine just one of those benefits: Medical insurance.

The company may tell you they have medical insurance. What they have and what you may think you're going to get can be two very different things. Ask yourself some questions.

- Is the coverage only on the employee, or for both the employee and his family?

- What is the coverage? 100%? 80%? Less?

- What is the deductible portion? $100.00? $200.00? $300.00. More?

- What is covered? (Be aware CHAMPUS is one of the most liberal programs in existence insofar as what conditions are covered.)

- Is dental coverage included? (How much and what conditions?)

- Is optical coverage included? (Examination only or eyeglasses as well?)

- Are prescription drugs on an outpatient basis covered?

- Are outpatient visits to a doctor covered?

- Are physical examinations covered?

- Are pre-existing conditions covered? If not, when do they become eligible for coverage?

- Is maternity care covered?

You could probably add questions to the list. An employer can arrange for very limited group medical insurance for employees. Still, he can say he gives medical insurance as a benefit. To have your dependents covered you may end up having $70.00 a month deducted from your paycheck to pay for their health insurance coverage alone. Few of us understand the complex language of insurance policies. Medical insurance policies are no exception. The point is, there is an extensive menu of items available for the insurer to choose from. Each item added increases the cost. Know what you're getting.

When comparisons are made between military service benefits and civilian industry benefits, the comparison is most probably made with companies of Fortune 500 rank. Be aware that most medium and small companies will have trouble matching those benefit packages.

You will run into evaluation problems similar to those in medical insurance coverage when examining the benefits of disability insurance coverage and retirement plans. A company may tell you they have a retirement plan, but how much good will a $100.00 a month annuity do you at age 60? You would be wise to examine what your vested rights are in a retirement program.

If the company has not explained the benefit package, you should take time before accepting the job to study and evaluate it. You will have no one to blame but yourself if you accept on the spot and later discover that the benefit package wasn't what you thought it was. That goes for every benefit down to what items are paid on relocation and what the provisions are in the retirement program. You can over-do your probing, but reasonable questions should receive straightforward answers.

Added now to your things to research if you want to be well prepared in job search is the matter of benefits. You don't have Congress looking out for your benefits in civilian employment as you have had in the military. You're on your own. Be prepared. Be informed.

SUMMARY

It would be unwise of you to adopt a preconceived salary level for your civilian job search. There are too many variables to consider in what constitutes a fair salary for the job you will ultimately land. The supply and demand for your skills and knowledge is probably the greatest determining factor in the salary you will receive.

Salary negotiation is not always possible. When it is, your negotiating skills will enable you to negotiate the best possible salary. Your good judgment should tell you when negotiating limits are reached. To press issues further will not serve in your best interests.

Benefit packages vary widely in civilian industry. It is extremely important to understand the provisions of existing benefit programs. A simple statement of an available benefit can mislead you to assuming the best. You must be prepared to wade through a jungle of programs to understand what really is being offered. That is why it is important not to accept a job until you understand what is being offered.

ENCOURAGEMENT

You are now aware of some of the most important aspects to consider in salary negotiation and benefit packages. By not being over anxious to discuss salary, your position will be enhanced as a knowledgeable negotiator.

Chapter 10

<u>PROFIT VS. MISSION</u>

<u>INTRODUCTION</u>

We have all heard about the necessity of completing the assigned military mission. Broken down to the smallest component of military organization, the total resources of capital, equipment, and manpower are committed to completing the assigned mission, whatever it may be. At times it becomes necessary to make hard and seemingly cruel decisions in the military to complete the mission. Equipment and even valuable manpower must at times be sacrificed to attain the goal.

In the corporate world, all the resources of capital, equipment, and manpower are committed to generating a **profit** — and don't **ever** forget it! In the civilian business world sacrifices in terms of human resources are probably much more common than in the military. If losses are draining available capital and if a profit is not made over a certain period of time, heads roll. The president and/or others in the chain of command are told to have their desks cleaned out by the end of the day. For them there will be no second chance to make it right. They may have seen their termination coming but didn't quite know when their actions (or inaction) caused them to cross the fine line between job security and job search. It is on such an occasion that others in the chain of command, from the top down to the lowest paid, can suffer for top management's poor performance.

THE BOTTOM LINE

The vast majority of firings or layoffs are brought on by poor performance and/or poor profits. It may be that the person affected was doing a splendid job and had no direct authority for the decision that brought on the losses. Nevertheless, the basic reasons of poor performance and/or poor profits as a result of **someone's** actions brought on the purge.

Cruel? Yes.

Fair? For some affected, no.

Universal? Almost.

Necessary? From a hard, empirical business standpoint — absolutely.

What is difficult for many people to understand and accept, right or wrong, is that the bottom line of business is profit as the ideal, and survival as the least acceptable level of performance. The less a company is able to absorb losses, the tougher the standards of performance become. When its very survival is at stake, a company's overhead is cut as quickly and severely as necessary. Be aware that salaries are usually the single largest overhead expense. Management salaries, if generous, become prime targets for elimination.

The foregoing observations are not made to emphasize the negative aspects of civilian employment. Their purpose is to "drive home" to the reader, as candidly as possible, the aspects of profitability and survival in the scheme of civilian business and employment. Just as the military person reacts appropriately to threats of survival, so does the businessman. The businessman can be every bit as ruthless in survival techniques as can the military person.

In the larger companies the supporting infrastructure will, to a certain degree, mask the aspects of the necessity for profit to a large number of employees. This is both good and bad. It is good because many in the chain of command are not given the responsibility for overall profits or the authority to influence key decisions that affect profits. It's bad because their lack of appreciation for the necessity of profit in business robs them of their sense of worth to the company in attaining those profits. It's kind of like the problem the military has in motivating those on mess duty to good performance. Their contribution is, within a larger context, important and necessary to the completion of the mission. However, the person performing the task often does not consider his contribution as being significant and important to completing the overall mission. But just as a military organization does not function without food, neither does a business prosper without the contributions of all of its employees.

It is a sad fact that many dedicated, efficient, hard-working employees can become victims of a purge brought about by poor management at the top. Understanding the necessity for profits during those times does not take away the sting of losing one's job. The realization that your contribution was not the cause but instead probably helped delay the purge will permit you to leave with your pride intact — and that is important.

In privately held firms where no quarterly or annual reports are issued, there is no concrete way for an outsider to know the profit or loss picture. However, there are classical tell-tale signs of poor profits. One of the most visable signs of heavy losses is a deep across-the-board purge of human resources.

One of the things you want to look for in a company where you seek employment is its profitability picture. If it is not good, try to find out from people from outside the company who are in a position to know if new management has just taken over. You could be positioning yourself for disaster if present management has been struggling to keep things afloat. Conversely, you may be able to attach yourself to a rising star with a new manager and enjoy the benefits of the ascent.

In effect, many people in organizations become beneficiaries of good management, or victims of poor management without realizing it until it is too late. Not all successful managers are loved, but it's a safe bet they are profitable.

If you have a fairly good understanding of business economics before you enter the civilian job market, you will be much better prepared to understand some of the things you will see and experience. If not, you may have a difficult time indeed trying to rationalize some of the things that go on. Understanding some of the basics of business economy will help take away some of the anxiety and hidden fears you may have about employment in the business world. At the least, the knowledge will alert you to a potentially precarious situation.

SUMMARY

Whatever the job you land in private business, be continually aware of what drives the activity. Profit. Lose sight of that underlying necessity in business and you beg for trouble. It's the one reality you can count on in private business.

ENCOURAGEMENT

Don't let the lack of knowledge of basics in business frighten you. Just about everyone learns them the hard way -- through experience. Try to have fun when you're learning them.

Chapter 11

THE ELEMENTS OF STRESS

INTRODUCTION

Virtually every job hunter experiences some stress. Some people accept job change in a matter-of-fact manner and adjust easily to changing or new situations. Others have trouble coping with the situation and essentially become ineffective job candidates. Few of us can make a job change without experiencing some stress. The very necessity to report for a job interview is enough to cause some people to enter into an excited and sometimes fearful state.

Whether stress is involved in a job search or change of job depends a lot on the individual himself. The person's qualifications, his financial condition, his self confidence, and his ability to adjust to unfamiliar conditions are all potential contributors to stress.

Good planning can help reduce the stresses in job search but will not completely eliminate them. An awareness of the stresses will help you cope. In some cases, the only way to diagnose the stress is through identification of the symptoms that accompany it. The following will help you become aware of some of the most common stresses experienced during a job search.

TYPES OF STRESS

Emotional

Among the various emotional crises one can experience during their life time, loss of one's job rates very high in stress quotient. It rates with death in the family, divorce, and bankruptcy.

The same type of spillover consequences that other high stress situations cause are present in the loss of one's job. That loss can be externally imposed as in a firing or it may be a voluntary separation. Nevertheless, stresses still are present. The status quo has been shattered. Routine changes. A period of evaluation and reflection sets in. You have stress!

The emotional impact of loss or change of jobs is tremendous. The factors bringing on the stress and the symptoms which manifest themselves are awesome unless you're prepared to face them. Until you've experienced unemployment, your appreciation of the attendant stresses will be muted. Don't overestimate your ability to cope with them. Recognize their capability to harm you and do your best to understand and deal with them. Then they cannot overwhelm you.

Financial

There are few people, indeed, who have not experienced financial stress. When financial stress results in the fear of not being able to provide for the basics of living such as food, clothing, and shelter, it becomes a very serious matter. A person loses his "normal" way of thinking and acting and goes into a survival mode. Being in a survival mode can work wonders on motivation but the penalties paid in stress are heavy.

There are other stresses beyond financial stress which may be somewhat less debilitating but will be of sufficient challenge so that every attempt should be made to reduce financial stress. The three key factors in your ability to reduce financial stress require planning. These three key factors are:

- Have sufficient funds to guarantee survival for a reasonable period of time

- Have a budget plan which reduces expenditures to only the necessities

- Have a plan to eliminate or reduce the period of unemployment

Assuming that you're prudent enough to assure the above efforts, let's look at some realistic financial stresses experienced by virtually every job changer.

There is the immediate necessity to re-evaluate your life style. You must eliminate the fat in your budget for those expenditures which are made with your disposable income. Purchases of luxuries, eating out, and planned vacations are obvious targets for elimination. The less your reserves are able to absorb such expenditures, the sooner you should eliminate them.

If an individual or a family can accept these cuts gracefully and endure them for the length of time necessary, the stress is reduced. More typically, it takes the impact of unpaid bills and crisis money management before the cuts are grudgingly accepted. By then, however, fear, frustration, anger, and feelings of inadequacy have set in and the symptoms of financial stress take their toll.

The fear of losing one's possessions through inability to meet monthly payments becomes serious when the roof over the family's head is involved. The loss of pride in losing a home is bad enough. Where you will live next becomes a real problem.

The immediate necessity of altering life styles has an effect on each member of the family. Old habits die hard. If youngsters are affected, their lack of realization that the source of funds has dried up only adds fuel to the fire. Family arguments between man and wife most often involve money, sex, or lack of appreciation for the other person. These powerful influences can shatter a marriage quickly.

Financial stress, therefore, comes in many forms. The frustration of being unable to remove the cause of the stress, namely, lack of money, only brings on more frustration.

<u>Ego</u>

Each of us has a perception of our own relationship or relative position vis-a-vis the demands of our social and physical environment. Inject a factor which affects that perception unfavorably and there is stress.

In the development of modern society all the trappings of ego building have been added which give us goals against which we can compare our own performance. Basic survival has few elements of ego. The mind and body are too involved in mere survival to assimilate a complex system of ego building. There are things beyond basic survival which society has established and which we internalize as being necessary that cause us trouble in terms of ego. Earning power, title, educational level, possessions, and authority over others are at the top of the list of ego builders. Social relationships and acceptance by others are still other ego builders which we nurture and protect.

So many factors of ego are affected by one's job that losing a job becomes a traumatic experience. Being in a job which gives little ego satisfaction is somewhat better than no job at all. It provides for basic survival and a base for ego building.

When a person is unemployed many of the reinforcements of ego building are removed and he must operate on residual trappings. In some cases, these trappings can be considerable and help sustain the person until reinforcement arrives.

A healthy, properly directed ego is good and necessary for a person's well being in modern society. Ego-building and maintenance, however, go hand in hand with confidence building. Shatter one, and the other suffers.

Lack of Confidence

The confidence we have in our own knowledge and abilities is paramount to job success. It permits us to take on tasks which we would otherwise avoid as being beyond our capabilities.

The longer a person is unemployed the less confident he is in his own abilities. In this situation, the mind is playing a "dirty trick," as it were, on the person. His abilities are no less than they were when he was employed. Unless they involve a complex skill which requires frequent exercise, his abilities remain the same. It's just that the symptoms of stress overpower the individual's confidence in his abilities.

Lack of confidence is sometimes brought about by lack of demand for the knowledge and skills possessed by the individual. But if his knowledge and skills are re-discovered, a miraculous transformation takes place in the confidence of the individual.

If a job seeker must present his knowledge and skills against requirements which are not allied or if his skills are inadequate to the task, his confidence in his skills is reduced. The stress of inadequacy is heaped on lack of confidence and the problem is compounded.

A job seeker lacking confidence in his own abilities will not excite the prospective employer. He is looking for an employee who has the confidence in himself which will enable him to make a positive contribution to the profit picture through competent performance of duties. If you come across as lacking that confidence, your chances of being hired are slim indeed.

Once a person's confidence in his abilities is reduced, strange psychological and even physiological symptoms occur. Psychologically he becomes depressed and evasive or, he may take the opposite tack and become arrogant and defensive. In either case, his effectiveness in a job search is reduced. He can be reduced to a shy, stammering individual completely out of character. He won't look the interviewer in the eye and fixes his gaze upon the floor or a remote object. At this stage, he is a candidate for psychological counseling. His job search may have to be deferred to allow him time to regain his confidence.

Loss of Identity

For those military people retiring after years of service, there is the potential for stress developing because of loss of identity. The structured environment of military service has provided them with a firm identity within the framework of rank, organization, and service. They wear the same uniform day in and day out, year after year. They are accorded the courtesies and perquisites associated with their rank and job assignment. They work, communicate, and socialize with people who understand their language and respect their position. Suddenly, upon retirement, all this changes.

Some people have trouble letting go of those things which they understand and can relate to. The civilians they encounter may neither recognize nor particularly respect their past accomplishments. The daily reinforcement of their identity ceases and they become confused, frightened and disoriented. They have stress and they don't quite know how to cope with it.

If they are really having trouble adjusting, the best thing they could probably do is seek counseling. The next best course of action would probably be to take some time off and evaluate their new environment. By taking time off and not plunging directly into a new job, they give themselves time to make the transition and adjust to civilian life at a slower pace. They do not have to give up any of their values, but they may have to find new ways of expressing them in the different environment. The hardest part may be that they not live in the past. They must find new challenges and a new identity. Sometimes that takes time, and patience is probably not their strongest attribute.

If the person is achievement motivated, the problem will probably resolve itself quicker than if the drive for achievement is missing. In any case, they should begin the search for a new identity which need not satisfy anyone but themselves. That is probably what is going to take the longest time for them to realize. They are so accustomed to pleasing a system with well defined norms that when that system is removed they lose their ability to substitute anything for it.

In such a case they should ask themselves the questions, "What are the things I have to offer and who could use them?" Ultimately, they must look to themselves for the answers. The thing they should realize is that **they do** have much to offer, they just haven't taken the time to identify those things in terms of a market. Using good research they can identify potential markets and find a new identity.

They will still have to adjust to their new identity but the fact that they are making an effort to find it will be half the battle. Let go of the past. Push on to new challenges. You can handle it!

SUMMARY

The mind and body are complex organisms. Even psychologists cannot always understand the reasons for some things our minds do. They can, however, recognize symptoms which are brought about by some underlying problem. The psychological and physiological stresses brought on by unemployment or job change can have an adverse effect. Your effectiveness in a job search can be reduced by these stresses. You may not be able to avoid the stresses but an understanding of their presence can help you adjust your behavior during the critical times of presentation of your qualifications to the prospective employer and the job interview. Once hired, many of the symptoms of stress will rapidly disappear along with the stresses you've experienced. The transition from a military career to civilian life can be traumatic for some people. The important thing to remember is that you have much to offer someone. A new identity awaits you. Don't be afraid of it. Go after it!

ENCOURAGEMENT

Short periods of unemployment can be refreshing and provide for necessary rest and relaxation. With good financial and job search planning, stress can be reduced to a minimum.

Chapter 12

THE RETIREE

INTRODUCTION

Military retirees entering the civilian job market have some distinct advantages over those completing shorter periods of service. On the other hand, there are some disadvantages in the form of prejudices that may be encountered because they are completing a long term of military service. The advantages are permanent; the prejudices can be overcome. Patience will be your greatest ally; impatience will be your greatest enemy.

More than the separating junior officer or junior enlisted person, the retiree will have difficulty in understanding why, in many cases, civilian employers just cannot seem to relate military experience to their business. The reason for this inability is that few civilians realize how well, and to what extent, military services train their managers in the latest management theories and practices. Too few civilian employers have an appreciation of just what you are capable of doing. You need the chance to show them.

ADVANTAGES

Retirement Pay

A distinct advantage you will have during a job search is your monthly cushion of retirement pay. It will reduce the financial pressures on you. It will enable you to spend more time in a search if necessary. The senior 30-year retiree might even be able to live on his retainer, but most others will have to find some sort of supplemental income to survive and to keep pace with inflation.

Another advantage retirement pay will offer is the salary level you will need in a job. You may be able to fulfill a life-long dream to work in a certain job, even if it means starting at the bottom of the pay ladder. If you land a well-paying job, you can start enjoying some of the things you probably have sacrificed during your climb in military pay and rank.

Experience

You carry with you into civilian life some of the best experience your potential employer will ever find. Combined with current technical knowledge, your collective knowledge of the evolutionary development of your speciality area makes you a walking encyclopedia. You probably know what works and what doesn't work in your specialty because you have **had** to make it work in the past. If things had fallen apart, you wouldn't have lasted to retirement. In short, you are a proven performer by virtue of your longevity in military service.

Leadership

You are a seasoned leader. You have had leadership training which is unsurpassed by anyone's definition and standard. You have had to practice leadership in the most difficult of environments. The judgment and maturity you exercised in the execution of your military position would be a challenge to any civilian. Having set an example, you did not permit yourself the luxury of easing it. You know how to motivate people and understand that by treating them right you can still maintain standards.

Survivability

You're a survivor. You and your family have proven that it is possible to overcome adversity and hardship. Often, at your military job, with inadequate levels of manpower and materials, you were called upon to perform nearly impossible tasks. Personality differences took second place to cooperation and teamwork. You faced the unpleasant and overcame it. If need be, you can do it all again. You know how to survive.

Ability to Adapt

Anyone who has spent a full career in military service has learned to adapt to change. At times, it may have been necessary for you to change your career path virtually overnight. For example, a change in assignment would have you in a line job one day and a staff job the next and you were given little time to master the requirements of a new job. In such cases, it was necessary to adapt to new duties, people, and conditions quickly and efficiently. There are few civilians who have experienced as many traumatic changes as you. Your ability and experience in adapting to change will serve you well in civilian life.

Work Stability

Any employer should welcome a retired military person as one with uncommon work stability and loyalty. Job hoppers turn employers off. You're the epitome of stability. Learn to sell that trait.

DISADVANTAGES

Retirement pay, experience, leadership, survivability, ability to adapt, stability and many other features of a military career are advantages you carry to the civilian job market. Unfortunately, not every employer has an appreciation for these advantages. In fact, there are features of a military career which can, or could, serve as disadvantages to you in the civilian job market. It all depends on the employer if your military career will be an advantage or disadvantage to you in your job search. Now, let's look at possible disadvantages to you as a military retiree.

Retirement Pay

Is this a contradiction? Can retirement pay be both an advantage and disadvantage? The answer depends on the employer. Retired military people rightfully acquire a sense of outrage when a prospective employer uses retirement pay as a factor in salary determination or negotiation. This practice seems most prevalent in areas of heavy concentration of retired military personnel. Some employers have the audacity to compute retirement pay from current pay charts and then use this information to determine how much he can adjust a salary downward for a retired military person he is considering as an employee. This is clearly a discriminatory practice. You would have grounds for a civil lawsuit if it happens to you and you can prove it. Don't stand for it!

Your retirement pay should have absolutely no bearing on the salary you are paid for a job. There are thousands upon thousands of other job searchers who have annuities from companies or organizations who escape the seemingly automatic reaction retired military people receive from the employer regarding retirement pay. Military retirement pay has become such a public issue that you often will hear discussions about it.

The best approach to the matter of retirement pay is not to discuss it. However, if the subject is brought up by the employer, it is probably best to make a statement to the effect that, "I can't live on it," or, "It's all committed, what there is of it." If the employer pursues the issue, set him straight. Tell him that you don't feel your retirement pay should be part of the discussions and that it is an aspect of your personal finances. That should get through to him that it doesn't belong in the discussions.

Age

Contrary to Equal Employment Opportunity (EEO) laws, employers do discriminate because of age. It is very difficult to prove that your skills and experience equal those of other applicants for a given job. Age alone does not entitle one to a job. The person must have the requisite skills and experience equal to other applicants. But, in many cases, you can turn age into an advantage. Large companies are usually aware of the rights of the protected age group in Equal Employment Opportunity laws. That portion of the law provides for equal opportunity for those in the 40 to 65-year age group, mandating that they cannot be discriminated against by reason of age. However, many medium and small size companies are not aware of this portion of the law.

In such a situation, express to the employer that you want the job and that he will be getting experience, judgment, maturity, and leadership in your services. Also, politely point out that your employment may help him to fulfill a requirement for a protected age group employee on his payroll. This simple statement of your awareness of discrimination because of age, without expressing an implied threat, may tip the scales in your favor.

Military Discipline

Military discipline is an abhorrence to many civilians. Many view retired military people as individuals who are automatons themselves, and unduly harsh disciplinarians. They may question your flexibility in situations where orders alone will not bring the desired results.

Businessmen can be very autocratic and harsh disciplinarians in their own way. If they yield ultimate authority in the company, there is no one to put a restraint on their actions. If an employer has ever worked under such a boss, he probably harbors fear of your potential for administering discipline. You don't want to appear to be a milksop; neither should you overemphasize your disciplinarian role in the military.

If employers realized that the vast majority of retired military have long ago learned the lessons of tempered, even-handed discipline, they wouldn't fear your potential. They would respect it for what it is.

Loyalty and Job Security

Who would ever think your sense of loyalty and job security would be a disadvantage in civilian employment? Only this time it's not a disadvantage to the employer and he certainly won't view it as such. The disadvantage is to you, personally, as an employee.

You have been well indoctrinated in loyalty. Your strong loyalty to country, service, organization, superiors, and your men are admirable traits. However, this strong sense of loyalty can harm you in civilian employment if it's misdirected. You may associate yourself with a company that's going nowhere or one in the throes of bankruptcy. With misdirected loyalty, you will stay on to the bitter end. This sense of loyalty will not permit you to abandon the sinking ship and strike out for personal survival.

The superior in whom your promotion possibilities rest may be a "turkey," but you remain loyal to him long past the point common sense tells you to move on. Your sense of loyalty tells you to support him and eventually things will work out for the best. Too many military retirees have experienced this phenomenon to advance it simply as a postulate. It is fact, supported by abundant proof.

Your sense of security in terms of stable employment with a steady paycheck, staying at the job until you earn maximum benefit, just reinforces this sense of loyalty. Your view of loyalty and security may be excessive to enable you to make a change when all indicators point to a change.

Many retirees go through traumatic job changes when it finally dawns on them that their loyalty is keeping them in an untenable situation. They agonize over the decision even if it is obvious they should change. It must be that they feel they are compromising their loyalty. Perhaps there is no way the point can make sense to you until you've experienced it. At least you have been made aware of it. You're not a traitor if you change employers. It's done every day by thousands of others.

The disadvantages of being retired from the military in your job search and eventual employment are things that can be overcome. Your awareness of their potential to harm you is the first step in overcoming them. Now let's discuss some other aspects of job search and employment for the military retiree.

CHANGING JOBS

It may be that you already are retired and have purchased this book in order to gain some pointers on job searching. If so, the same planning and research recommended for those anticipating retirement is an appropriate approach.

Since you have already become familiar with civilian industry to some degree, you can compress the planning and research time frame into weeks. The newness of daily contact with only civilians will have passed and you will be at ease and more confident in your search. Above all, don't be distressed that you're making a change. You're not alone.

It would be interesting to make a study of how many retired military people are still in the first job they acquired after their retirement. It probably would be a safe wager to estimate that a majority of them are at their second or third job. Just what can be attributed to this job changing is problematic. Could it be a lack of initial planning and research to identify their niche? Or, could it be unfulfilled expectations of salary, title, responsibility, or security? Whatever it is, it's disquieting to those anticipating retirement. They may find some comfort in the realization that they will be in good company. Many of their predecessors have found it necessary to change jobs, even though they may have thought that was something they never would have to do.

Civilians today are changing jobs at a frequency never before experienced by industry. The demand for technical knowledge, in particular, enables people with technical skills to identify new jobs while still employed, thereby reducing the trauma of a change.

One must be careful, however, how often and for what reasons he changes jobs. Less than two to three years in your last job may make the potential employer suspicious of your reason for change. A firing, for whatever reason, bodes ill for the job changer. A poor reference from an employer will guarantee you a tougher time in finding a new job.

A change every three to five years for upward mobility, greater challenge, or other good reason, generally will be viewed by potential employers as reasonable longevity with each company. If a downward trend in responsibility or pay is evident, the employer will rightfully suspect you have a problem.

Military retirees often obtain employment far afield from their military specialization. This job exploration increases the chance for dissatisfaction. It may take one or two changes for them to crystalize their interests, find the right opportunity, and to acknowledge some of the unpleasant aspects inherent in civilian employment. As long as you haven't burned any bridges during a change, potential employers will usually understand your situation.

The best way to make a change is to have the new job arranged before you resign from your current one. As a survivor, you can last out just about any situation until you identify a new opportunity. When you depart a company, do it gracefully because your reputation will follow you. If you tell the boss off when you depart, you can expect a bad reference. It isn't worth it. Keep that employer believing you love him and that you're the greatest, even if it hurts to do it. You never know when you may meet him again or in what capacity he may be in the future.

Any employer who hires people without first checking references usually will regret their omission. Many people can put on a good show during an interview but their track record will not support their claims. An employer has to be burned only once before he learns his lesson — the hard way.

CHALLENGE AND RESPONSIBILITY

You have become accustomed to challenge. With each new assignment has come new challenges and responsibilities. Rank all but guaranteed suitable assignment to challenge your abilities. You had to step in and take charge, learn fast, and make things happen as you believed they should.

You may have a difficult time finding a job which you believe adequately challenges your abilities. It is important that you realize that the chances of finding organizational structures with missions similar to those in which you gained your experience in the military are somewhat limited. The structure and activity in organizations which can support a manager of your caliber will require that the manager possesses certain knowledge that you may not have had the opportunity to acquire.

The armed services provide for unprecedented opportunities in responsibility. From the time you were appointed an NCO, or commissioned a junior officer, you have carried responsibility equivalent to, or in excess of, the vast majority of civilian supervisors and managers. The scope of your responsibilities and numbers of people under your charge increased with each higher rank. The sudden reduction in responsibility upon changing jobs may leave you with a feeling of restlessness and lack of challenge. However, challenges and responsibilities await you, but they may be in a different form than you are accustomed. Therein lies the potential for transition trauma.

Many of the things you attempt to evaluate will be difficult to rationalize because there is no military comparison to it. Just as the civilian who comes on your base or ship is awed by all that is going on, it will hit you how differently things are done in civilian businesses.

In many cases, because of these differences, you may not be prepared or qualified to assume a level of responsibility you were accustomed to in the military. You essentially have all the management and leadership skills necessary to do the job. You just lack knowledge and experience in the civilian environment. If civilian employers had the proper appreciation for how fast you could adapt and how much you already know which is transferable or intuitive because of your experience, military retirees wouldn't encounter the problems they sometimes do in gaining the employer's confidence from the beginning.

There is the potential for you to become irritated while trying to gain certain knowledge in a given business. This is because some employers have a tendency to make you jump through every preliminary hoop to advance. You're required to spend weeks or months at what you could learn and assimilate in hours or days in order to satisfy established programs for advancement. You may be spoon fed information. That would be alright if it was directed to learning the business. Instead, much of the information will be associated with basic leadership and supervisory skills which you learned long ago and have been practicing for years. Instead of briefing you on some aspect of the business which you will supervise but will not be performing yourself, you may be required to perform the task for a seemingly endless period of time. This supposedly will be to ensure that you really understand it. Your patience may grow thin and you may begin to believe your intelligence is being insulted.

The typical first reaction to such a situation is that you will be happy to go through a training program to learn what's going on. But too often employers underestimate your potential for learning. The fact that you possess superior management skills which can be quickly adapted to their situation escapes them. You acquire a sense of urgency, and therein lies one potential for you to change jobs in order to find something more challenging. The employer just won't move you as fast as you believe you should advance.

The employer who understands the depth of knowledge, experience, leadership, and management skills the retired military person possesses and then channels that potential in his business properly within a reasonable time frame, will have a winner on his team. If they fail to recognize and challenge that potential properly, they will lose him.

The way you can position yourself for the proper challenge with a potential employer is to know his business. Research! Research! Research! Go after the information you need about a potential employer the way you did in the first weeks of each new assignment you had in the military. Unless you can convince the employer that your knowledge and experience is adaptable to his business, you may find yourself in a job well below your potential. They may rate your other skills at the level of your knowledge of their business.

DIFFERENT CHALLENGES

Because it is sometimes so difficult for the military retiree to find challenges which match previous experience, you may have to seek out a very different challenge. It is in this situation that two important aspects of job search be applied:

- Know yourself
- Don't dismiss any job out-of-hand as being inappropriate

In evaluating your past experience you will discover trends. It doesn't necessarily take a personal preference inventory test to identify your interests. What you do have to do is identify civilian occupations that match your interests. There are broad classifications of civilian jobs for which you may possess innate abilities but you are unfamiliar with success indicators for those jobs. Sales is a perfect example. Many retired military people have innate characteristics of a successful salesperson. Achievement motivation, a good work ethic, ability to communicate well, imagination, persistence, good grooming, and many other traits for successful salesmanship are traits you may already possess. Don't dismiss sales as a possible occupation.

Most military retirees are good administrators. The biggest problem they have in identifying administrative jobs is their general idea of what they believe administration means in civilian industry. Ask any military person what he believes administration means and invariably he will say "personnel work." There are thousands of jobs in civilian business and industry of an administrative nature which have precious little in common with the personnel administrative field.

Ask a civilian what personnel work means and he will probably say, employment, labor relations, compensation, safety, EEO, Affirmative Action, OSHA, ERISA, recruitment, and all those other headaches.

The point is, ex-military seek out personnel jobs when they are probably more suited to jobs which require administrative skills that are not necessarily associated with pure **personnel** administrative functions. Even those who have had an assignment as Personnel Officer in the military are probably not qualified to assume civilian personnel management jobs. They are two different worlds. The very act of interviewing a prospective employee in civilian industry requires knowledge of Federal and state labor laws which are extensive in scope and loaded with potential lawsuits if violated. The personnel function has become highly segmented with specialities to the point that a good generalist is hard to find because of the knowledge required.

More appropriately, the retiree with a strong administrative bent should seek out jobs which require general administrative ability in handling paper work combined with management responsibility. The other abilities you probably possess such as directing people, and being a good communicator both orally and in writing, will enhance your competitive edge for administrative jobs.

Many retirees have found challenge and satisfaction in sales work as well as in jobs such as Association Director, large residential complex manager, or small office manager. There are hundreds upon hundreds of jobs which require general administrative ability combined with management skills. Don't dismiss a job out-of-hand as being inappropriate. Titles of jobs can be misleading. There are many retirees who have found challenge and satisfaction in being fund raisers for churches, colleges, and other institutions. There are thousands who have gone into business for themselves. You're a natural for that, if you're careful so that you know what you're doing. Put your imagination to work. A job awaits you if you will just exert the effort to find it. Remember, the odds are solidly against a job finding you.

SUMMARY

As a military retiree you enter the marketplace with both advantages and disadvantages. The disadvantages can be overcome. A change of jobs may be necessary before you find a challenge which suits you. Do not permit your sense of loyalty and job security to entrap you in an untenable situation which can be resolved by changing jobs. Line up a new job before leaving your current one.

Examine your motivations and interests. They point in the direction of job satisfaction. Don't dismiss any job out-of-hand as being inappropriate. Titles of jobs can be misleading to the job content. Investigate the job. You may be surprised how well it fits your desires.

ENCOURAGEMENT

Your predecessors have established an admirable reputation for the value of a military retiree as an employee. You represent the finest available on the job market.

Chapter 13

AGENCY ASSISTANCE

INTRODUCTION

There are various types of agencies that offer assistance in career counseling, job placement, and testing. Some of them operate under the auspices of Federal or state agencies at public expense. Others are strictly free enterprise businesses that operate to generate a profit. Few agencies are able to offer full service to the job searcher. One reason is because they may be restricted in the population they serve. Other reasons have to do with their inability to do so or the emphasis on which services they offer. It takes a great deal of time, effort, and specialized knowledge to do a complete job of testing, counseling, and training (if necessary). Added to this background work is the actual placement of an applicant in a job.

A single chapter in one book cannot cover all the types of agencies and services available to the job searcher. Therefore, only a few of the more commonly encountered agencies will be discussed in this chapter.

EXPECTATIONS

The sad fact of the matter is that regardless of what type of agency you have contact with, they will probably fall far short of your expectations for services rendered.

Disadvantaged people usually receive the most complete service by government agencies. Even then, the services are usually given under the sponsorship of a showcase program. Realistically, government agencies, universities, and private employment agencies offer limited services to the masses. Each type of agency can offer you certain services. Just remember when choosing which type of agency will represent you to not build your expectations too high. Each of them have certain strengths and weaknesses. Therefore, the best approach to using them is to capitalize on their strengths and forgive their weaknesses. By doing this, the help you get will offer encouragement in your job search. If you expect them to do it all for you, you're headed for disappointment.

GOVERNMENT AGENCIES

Government agencies, such as the Department of Labor's U.S. Employment Service Job Service and the Veteran's Administration may be capable of providing complete service. They have public funding available which enables them to staff their offices with the various specialists it takes to offer full service. The only problem with these organizations is that all the services cannot be provided for everyone hoping to utilize them. They would have to have tremendously increased staffs to do a complete job for everyone. They may state in their literature that all the services are available, but to receive them all is another matter. It just would not be practical because of the vast numbers of people applying, and the real necessity for each person to receive all services.

As is the case with so many government programs, you must know what to ask for, and have the courage to ask for it. Don't expect to walk into their offices, have the red carpet laid out for you and then have someone research just how many ways they can help you. Instead, you can expect lines and waits before talking to a counselor.

Talking with a counselor does not automatically gain you testing and other services. These will be determined on an individual basis. The Job Service's 2,500 offices nationwide cannot begin to do the job adequately. The hugh amount of people applying for help in finding a job overloads the system to the point where their advertised services are no more than statements of their charter. Their ability to fulfill their stated responsibilities is marginal.

PRIVATE EMPLOYMENT AGENCIES

There are thousands of private employment agencies operating throughout the United States. They may carry such names as Personnel Agency, Recruiting Agency, Search Firm, or any similar names. Many advertise "full service" while others offer specialized services. Some offer walk-in service while others operate on a "by appointment only" basis.

To the uninitiated, they present a bewildering array of fee arrangements and areas of specialization. Few job searchers really understand the way private employment agencies are organized, operate, and are regulated. They have a poor understanding of what they can expect in working with them. Therefore, some explanations are in order.

Overall Effectiveness

Today, private employment agencies are responsible for about two percent of all hires made annually in the United States. They represent a rather young industry since they first came into prominence shortly after World War II.

In terms of numbers of candidates using their services versus the number placed in jobs, the record of private employment agencies is dismal. No agency, government or private, fares well in that statistic. Part of the reason for the failure of agencies to garner a better statistical average in placement activity is that the people using their services do not understand how they operate. Let's see if we can unravel some of the mysteries surrounding private employment agencies so you will have a better understanding.

<u>Who Pays?</u>

Perhaps the placement fee is the first thing you should be aware of when dealing with an agency. Who pays it? You or the employer? Remember, private employment agencies are in business to make a profit. Someone has to pay the freight.

An agency can be either EPF (Employer Paid Fee) or APF (Applicant Paid Fee), or both EPF and APF. The industry had its beginning principally with APF agencies. Over the years the trend shifted and now favors EPF agencies.

The fee structures for both types of agencies vary widely. Most states regulate agencies and dictate fee schedules for APF agencies. The states view the job applicant as a consumer of services and therefore will regulate the fees which can be charged for service. Usually the fee is a percentage of monthly salary. Some APF agencies will charge as much as 155 percent of the first month's salary as the service fee, depending on the regulations their states have enacted. Most will charge maximum levels permitted by law. If you use an APF agency, you should read the contract you sign very carefully. It is enforceable in court.

State laws usually require the agency to give clear evidence in their advertising if they are APF, EPF, or both. This will enable you to choose the type agency with which you will deal. Terms like "All Fees Paid" will tell you they are an EPF agency.

In EPF agencies, the employer pays the fee to the agency for placing the candidate with their company. Fees charged the company will vary widely. Usually the determining factor is what the market will bear. In some areas, a low of 10 percent of the annual salary is the fee. Usually the fee is closer to an even percent of annual salary. For example, if the person placed will receive an annual salary of $24,000.00, the fee is calculated as:

$$\$24,000.00 \times 24\% = \$5,760.00$$

The fee schedules of most agencies peak at 30 percent of annual salary regardless of whether or not the salary of the individual placed is greater than $30,000 per year. If the market will tolerate higher rates, fee schedules are adjusted accordingly. Some agencies can command up to 50 percent of an annual salary as the placement fee. When a company needs a key executive, the fee is incidental to the profits he can generate. If the company is millions of dollars in the red and the executive can turn it around to millions in profit in a short period of time, the search fee is a very good investment indeed.

Employer's View

No company or organization likes to pay an agency fee. They do it out of necessity. Recruiting is a costly procedure in terms of advertising dollars and management time. If a company runs a recruitment ad in newspapers and trade journals and does not attract the person they desperately need, what is their alternative? They can put the word out in their industry by word of mouth, or possibly get referrals from their own employees or the government job service. Once these sources are exhausted they have the alternatives of calling a private employment agency or doing without the person needed. Employers have come to realize that a key employee quickly pays for his own salary and the employment fee as well. The reaction time of a good recruiter is something they have come to depend upon. The employer knows which agency or recruiter understands the company's requirements and often will use that agency or recruiter to the exclusion of others. The recruiter, in effect, becomes a part of their management team. He is being paid to do the job and do it well.

  Agencies most often can perform the recruiting task more effectively than the company or organization can themselves. It is the agency's business to recruit and identify talent. They are not restricted from contacting competitors of their client company to recruit talent already qualified in systems or product knowledge. As a third party agent, the recruiter has a much freer hand in recruiting candidates on a confidential basis without compromising the company's needs. There are times when management wants the search to remain absolutely confidential. At other times, management has neither the time nor a person with recruiting expertise on his staff to recruit the talent they need. Agencies will pre-screen and do reference checks on candidates. This saves time and money for the client company if the agency does the job well.

Applicant's View

No applicant likes to pay an agency a fee to find them a job. They do so out of necessity. If the applicant can get an EPF agency to find him a job it costs him nothing. He will naturally try their services first. When he is desperate to find work and has exhausted all his own contacts, he may feel the fee is justified in order to get a job. In a tight job market with limited skills to sell, this may be the applicant's only alternative when his own search efforts produce no results.

The APF agency will usually arrange for the fee to be paid in monthly installments. This may take some of the sting out of paying a fee.

Selecting An Agency

One of your first considerations in selecting an agency to work with will probably involve payment of the fee. Naturally you would prefer that the employer pays the agency fee. But is paying the placement fee yourself ever justified? Only you can make that determination. Some things to consider in making this determination are your own marketability, the immediacy of your need, and your ability to pay the fee.

Here is where the greatest misunderstanding of the function of the private personnel agency comes into play. Ask yourself the basic questions, "Who is going to work the hardest for whom, and for what reasons?" The answers are multi-faceted, but the answers will help you understand agency charters.

Private employment agencies are in business to make a profit. The dispensing of free services to companies or applicants is not in their charter. In the case of applicants, the agency is essentially forced to identify the applicant's marketability or ability to pay a fee. In the case of employers, the service the agency provides necessitates that they do their homework. In a typical search, for example, all the work of recruiting the applicant, matching his background to the opportunity, and reference checking must be done even if the applicant is not hired. The company must have indicated a willingness to pay a fee before the candidate is presented. Therefore, unless you or the employer has something to offer, the service you receive will be limited.

Many agencies will offer "full service" and approach that charter with full "lip service." In reality, you may receive full services only if you, as an applicant, clearly represent a potential placement. For the agency to give free, complete service in testing, counseling, and job placement to all applicants, regardless of qualifications, would not be a wise business practice. They would soon invoke the provisions of bankruptcy if they did it.

False advertising? Maybe so. The question of what constitutes "full service" to a given applicant has never been tested in the courts. Each case would have to be defended on its own merits and it is unlikely the case would ever go to trial. Caveat emptor (Let the buyer beware)!

Private employment agencies do perform a valuable service though. The unfortunate thing is that they cannot help everyone. The lack of public understanding of their charters is what causes them to be criticized for lack of performance.

Evaluate your own marketability when selecting an agency. If you are well qualified in a knowledge or skill that is in demand, an EPF agency will be pleased to help you. If you're willing to pay the fee, an APF agency will be more than willing to look for a job for you. An agency's willingness to work with you does not guarantee that they will find you a job. They are under no obligation to spend "X" amount of their time looking, or expending "Y" amount of effort in doing so. Usually they will expend the most effort on the most marketable candidate, and the most fillable job order.

EPF agencies work for only those companies that do, or are willing to pay a fee. As an applicant, you will become just as important to the agency as is the company if you are highly marketable or they have a position in which they believe they can place you. Their emphasis is on finding people for jobs, not jobs for people. APF agencies may work harder for you if you are marketable and willing to pay the fee. An employer is more likely to talk to a candidate if there is no fee involved that he must pay.

Another important consideration in selecting which agency you want to work with is the ability of the individual recruiter or counselor to give you proper service. Agencies carry their own reputations as overall performers in the industry but what it really boils down to is the ability of the **individual** recruiter with whom you are working.

Some agencies attempt to serve all industries and disciplines. They eventually gravitate toward specialization. When you choose an agency to work with, attempt to identify their areas of specialization. It saves everybody a lot of time and you won't be disappointed if they cannot help you.

Private employment agencies do not have strong reputations for hiring qualified personnel counselors. Their recruiters or counselors are hired more for sales ability than for personnel counseling skills. When they do find qualified counselors who possess sales ability, it is a real find. Too often, though, the counselors will realize that their duties involve selling more than counseling and that becomes a turn-off to them.

The training recruiters and counselors receive is almost exclusively devoted to salesmanship, not personnel counseling. They are taught to identify skills for the purpose of matching them with job specifications. The remainder of their training is usually devoted to recruiting techniques, understanding client company needs, overcoming objections by the candidate or company, closing a sale, and follow-up. They are mostly sales people, not qualified personnel counselors.

Therefore, if you need a strong salesperson to sell your skills and knowledge, you've probably contacted the right person. If you need a qualified personnel counselor to help you understand yourself, counsel you on career objectives, and guide you to certain realizations, you're probably not talking to the right person. Those services do not come cheap, and generally are not found in private employment agencies. You will have to determine for yourself if the individual counselor in the agency is satisfying your needs.

Working With Agencies

EPF agencies are organized in many different ways. Some will specialize in executive recruitment at the upper management levels. National leaders in executive recruitment such as the top three ranking

Korn/Ferry International, Heidrick and Struggles, and Spencer Stuart and Associates, are well known in executive circles. They are under contract by many firms to conduct executive searches. Most EPF agencies conduct searches on what is called a "contingency fee" basis. What that means is that the payment of the search fee is contingent upon them placing a qualified candidate in the position.

There are thousands of EPF agencies and hundreds of free lancers recruiting talent for industry. There are the large national franchised operations such as Management Recruiters, Dunhill Personnel Agencies, and Snelling and Snelling. Independent agencies far outnumber them and are located everywhere. Many agencies belong to large associations such as the National Association of Personnel Consultants. Association membership provides for mutual cooperation in exchanging job orders and candidates, conducting training seminars, as well as serving as a lobbying forum for legislation.

Thousands of one man shops, licensed and unlicensed, operate from offices or homes. While most states attempt regulation of the industry, few are able to control it well. Testing and licensing is required in most states. In some, all that is required to go into business is to hang up your shingle and, hopefully, make some placements.

APF agencies will happily make placements of management and middle management applicants. The problem arises because few higher level applicants are prepared to pay the fee associated with their placement. The fee can be very significant. The APF marketplace seems to be more in entry level, clerical, and other lower paying jobs. They still hold a large share of the market so apparently people are still willing to pay for the service. They do make it easy for the person who isn't prepared to put forth the effort to find their own job but is willing to pay someone to do it for them.

The thing to remember in working with agencies is that they generally know what's going on in the marketplace. They have extensive knowledge of industries in the area and talk to hiring officials on a daily basis. They are, in effect, brokers of talent. Some deal exclusively in the recruiting function and are not anxious to talk to walk-in applicants. Most, however, welcome well qualified applicants since it builds up their data base to fill existing and future job openings.

As an applicant you should be aware that agencies are not excited about working with a candidate who has sent his resume, or visited, every agency in the city. Select one or two agencies you feel can best meet your needs and give them a chance to market your background. Be honest when you are asked where you have applied. If you have applied at 50 to 60 companies in the area, few agencies will be interested in working with you.

Agencies can be very effective in arranging for interviews. They know the employer, his personality, and his needs. That recruiter, or counselor as they are often called, is a superior salesperson. They have been known to arrange for a candidate interview and cause him to be hired even after the applicant has contacted the company on his own and was turned away by someone in the front office!

If you use them as a "last resort" option, you will be so heavily exposed to the marketplace it leaves little for them to do in the short run. They will be inclined to market you only to a few companies you have not contacted and where there may be an opening. Then your application will be filed away for future consideration.

You are guaranteed to be dropped like a "hot potato" if they market you to a company that you have not listed as contacting, when you have done so. Should you eventually be hired by that company, the agency will not get a fee and you will be an anathema to them. Competition for applicants and job orders is tough among the agencies themselves. When they get an applicant or company that does not level with them, their business relationship ends immediately. It's not that all agencies are so totally ethical themselves. But why continue a business relationship where you have to compete against your own applicant or client while doubting their honesty?

Too few agencies have counselors who understand military backgrounds. If they do not see a direct analogy for your experience, they will not know how to market your background. They often do not recognize or have appreciation for your strengths based on military service. Find a counselor who has extensive military experience and he probably will be in the best position to help you. You may not be their easiest placement but chances are you're marketable if they understand what you've done.

CAREER COUNSELING FIRMS

There are a number of firms (not agencies) which offer in-depth career counseling. They will provide for testing for interest areas, sessions with psychologists, on going counseling sessions, and guidance in job search techniques. They cannot guarantee that you will find the job you're looking for but will guide you in identifying the career areas and markets for which you are best suited. Finding the job is essentially up to you once you know what you're looking for. All this they do — for a significant fee.

Many people have trouble evaluating and identifying their own skills, knowledge, strengths, and motivations. That's not surprising since many people feel dissatisfied with their work and the direction their career is going. Whether you want to spend the necessary money to help you understand yourself is entirely up to you as an individual. Just don't be too surprised if the results only confirm what you already suspected. The question to ask yourself once you've found out is, "What am I going to do about it?" You will have to take the action. Someone showing you ways to take the action may help you reach your goal. No one, really, is going to do it all for you.

Once you have found out what you are best suited for, you may not like the payoff in terms of available jobs and your earning power in that field.

There are thousands of frustrated amateur psychologists on the job market, for example. They really want to work "with people" and ideally they may be best suited for that type work. Reality in the marketplace, however, has them working in all sorts of jobs which only partially fulfill their desires. Will they ever be satisfied? Probably not!

There are times we must make tradeoffs in things we want to do. To be totally fulfilled in your career goals is something we all would like to experience. Too often in spite of our best efforts to reach them, we must accept something less than the ideal. Those who are truly motivated will often attain their goals. For each person realizing success in their chosen field, there are many still struggling to attain success. Success and fulfillment do not come overnight.

SUMMARY

There are various government and private employment agencies that can be of assistance to you in your job search. Your expectations of their ability to assist you may be based on a misunderstanding of their charters. Overall, their record in placing people in jobs when compared to the number of people using their services is dismal. That statistic can, to a good degree, be attributed to people not understanding their function.

No one, employer or applicant, likes to pay a placement fee. They do it out of necessity. If you, as an applicant, pay a fee for placement service, you will do it through an APF agency. In EPF agencies the fee is paid by the employer.

In selecting an agency to work with, make every attempt to understand the areas of specialization they work in. It will save you time and disappointment if they cannot help you. Cooperate with the agency for best results. They are there to help you if they can. Should you feel the need for in-depth career counseling, there are firms which specialize in that service. Be prepared to pay a fee for their services. You, personally, will still have to take the action to realize your goals once you identify what they are.

Agencies can be of real help in your job search but remember, nothing beats personal contact with the employer.

ENCOURAGEMENT

You now know more about private personnel agencies than the vast majority of those using their services. You can use them to advantage now that you understand their charter.

Chapter 14

STARTING YOUR OWN BUSINESS

INTRODUCTION

Many people have maintained a life-long dream of starting their own business. A perfect time to do so is upon completion of military service. For the retiree in particular, starting a business presents an interesting and challenging alternative to working for someone else. The assurance of their monthly retirement check to cover the basic costs of living enables them to consider this alternative.

The old adage that success in business is 10 percent inspiration and 90 percent perspiration holds true today just as it has over the years. For those with the energy and commitment to make a success of business, the opportunity awaits them.

There are pluses and minuses in owning your own business. It is imperative that you are aware of some of these before you start or buy a business. Hundreds of new businesses are started every day. For every successful and viable one, there are many that end up in bankruptcy and disappointment. Experience in business helps but does not guarantee success. Careful planning does more to assure success than does the availability of money. So if you start or buy a business, plan carefully and realistically.

MOTIVATION AND COMMITMENT

Different things motivate different people. Motivators such as money, recognition, independence, prestige, security, etc., are things to which most of us can relate. In business, such motivators serve as the base for our reasons for going into business. They give us goals to strive for and help us measure our success.

More important than the goals, however, is the commitment we must make to reach them. It takes a very strong commitment to succeed in business. There are many things you must learn which are not written in any book or for which no advice is readily available.

Regulations and taxes place tremendous burdens on the small businessman. They will often wonder if the rewards are worth the trouble and effort. As long as the goals appear attainable, a strong commitment will see the businessman through the rough times. It is when the goals are based on unrealistic expectations that he is in trouble. Too often the small businessman fails to prepare a business plan which would enable him to set realistic goals.

THE BUSINESS PLAN

A good business plan assesses every aspect of a proposed business before any investment is made or business conducted. Everything from incorporation and organization through long range planning is addressed. Financial projections, budgets, costs, marketing and sales projections are all developed and included in the plan.

Anyone can start a company by paying incorporation and licensing fees. To keep the company viable is the problem. With a good business plan you will increase your chances for success because you will have considered many of the factors which, when ignored, lead to business failure. Foremost among these factors is sound financial planning.

There are too many ingredients in a good business plan to address them all in this one chapter. Therefore, we shall concentrate on just four aspects. These four have been shown to be the largest contributing factors to small business failures. They are:

- Undercapitalization
- Financial Controls
- Market Research
- Expansion

<u>Undercapitalization</u>

A business plan should contain a conservative approach to start-up and operating expenses. It quickly becomes apparent that more money is necessary than was originally planned. Start small and be conservative. Money will go much quicker than you ever dreamed possible. Assume you must pay for everything, because you will.

It is far wiser to start a shoestring operation with good cash reserves than make a big splash for start-up image and then wonder where the first month's operating capital is going to come from.

If virtually all of your cash is committed for start-up, you're begging for trouble. Most businesses take two years to show a profit. That's all right if you're able to draw a management salary and have the business stay viable. But that is just an indication of how small a margin it is on which most small businesses operate. Any decline in business, unforseen expenses, or expansion efforts, can put you in a serious financial crisis if there are no reserves to back you. Because it is unlikely that you will include every potential expense in your business plan, you must plan for the unexpected.

Required office space, furniture, fixtures, or equipment should be leased or rented rather than purchased. To ensure viability, maintain cash reserves that will pay six months of the lease or rent payments. Purchase, lease, or rent only what is absolutely necessary to begin the business. The frills can be added later when they can be paid for out of corporate profits.

The overnight success of small businesses is the exception — not the rule. Even the success stories have a genesis of two to five years and a history of sacrifice. The "Pet Rock" and "Hula Hoop" successes were flukes based on a fad market. Successes? Certainly. But they were not the norm.

No amount of wishful thinking or rationalization will produce the cash necessary to keep a business going. If your business start-up is under capitalized and operating expenses are not planned for, your dream will be shattered. Keep it small, conservative, and viable.

Financial Controls

Financial control is equally as important as financial planning. The finest financial planning can be incorporated into a business plan but without adequate controls this planning is meaningless. The best financial control is simply: Don't spend it until you have it. The second best financial control is realizing you're spending too much and then forcing yourself to control future spending. In either case, fiscal discipline and cash control are required.

Budgeting helps with financial controls but there must be built-in controls that will not exceed budgeted amounts. Then, if revenues do not support the budgeted amounts, the built-in controls will modify the budget to keep costs in line. Complicated? To be sure. Necessary? Absolutely if you want to stay in business. The surest way to bankruptcy in business is to not understand or control costs.

If your understanding of budgeting, accounting, and cost control is weak, either go to school to increase your understanding or hire someone to do it. A good bookkeeper or accountant is worth his weight in gold. However, the discipline will still be up to you. A bookkeeper or accountant can help you set up controls and explain things so you know what action you must take to stay in fiscal control.

Financial controls make you face reality. The Holiday Inn chain has a perfect advertising slogan which is fully apropos in support of financial controls: "The best surprise, is no surprise."

An important aspect of financial control during start-up and operation of a small business is the matter of salaries paid. Typically the owner/manager grabs off the first monies coming in as, what is euphemistically called, a "management fee." That means salary. It matters not that expenses have been incurred and bills will be coming due. In his mind he has made a "profit," has earned it, and it is his just reward for his investment and effort. Wrong! In business, at least in the beginning, everyone else should be paid first. Cash in does not necessarily mean profits. The owner first must consider what liens there are against that cash before he takes any of it for himself. When a business is in the start-up phase it cannot stand the strain of paying a management fee to anyone.

When the company's financial problems become an integral part of the owner's personal financial problems, the business is operating under a handicap. The two are difficult for the small business owner to keep separate. When all the emotional aspects of family finances start impacting on the business, the business is in trouble.

If the business was undercapitalized to begin with and poor financial controls require an infusion of funds from an already strained family budget, the situation becomes intolerable for the owner. He has probably given personal guarantees to vendors for equipment leased or other services. In such cases, he becomes frantic and his business suffers because he cannot devote his full attention to it. Now you can begin to appreciate why so many small businesses fail because of under capitalization and lack of financial controls.

Remember these points:

- Keep your family and business finances separate and do not have one dependent upon the other. It is easier said than done but, nonetheless, essential to sound business practice.

- Don't commit all your funds to start-up with no reserves left for operating expenses.

- Put financial controls into effect at the onset of business.

- Don't draw a salary until everyone else has been paid. It's the conservative approach; the successful approach.

Market Research

It is easy to get excited about a product or service as a potential business. The perceived demand can generate such enthusiasm on your part that you hock your home and car to capitalize on the wonderful opportunity. It gets even more exciting and easier if someone else has already supposedly done the market research. Caution! All may not be what it **seems** to be. Again, it is the success stories that we've heard about that spark our excitement. Just don't act too fast. If the product or service seems feasible, research it thoroughly, then think about it some more. If, after a reasonable "cooling off" period, it still seems right, prepare a business plan.

To help put things in perspective, we'll draw on an analogy from a phenomenon common in the legal profession.

> The wronged party contacts his lawyer with a tale of unthinkable transgression against him which certainly is without precedent. The Counselor hears him out, reaches for a volume on case law, and reads out loud the decision on a case which almost exactly matches the situation. What do you know? Someone else **did** do it!

The fact that someone else thought about it, or even did it before, need not discourage you. It may still be a good idea. Maybe the others never followed through with action. It could be that such a business exists and they need some competition. Maybe those who tried and failed didn't do it right or lacked your enthusiasm and commitment.

Our own likes and needs most often take precedence over those of other people. That is why we can get excited about a product or service. Even if others share our likes and needs, there are still unanswered questions. Will they pay for it? How much will they pay for it? How many would pay for it? Can this be turned into a profitable business? You will need to do some market research to find the answers.

Sometimes it is easier to sell an idea than a product or service. Millions of dollars have been made and millions more have been lost trying to prove marketing ideas. As a small business man starting out you cannot afford to have a marketing survey conducted. One thing you can do, though, is try to find out if someone else has previously tried it, or is doing it now. If someone else has tried it, how successful were they? If there is no evidence of someone else trying it, you may want to do so.

One sure way to find out if there is a market for your business idea is to ask your friends and neighbors if they would buy the product or use the service. If the product or service is directed toward businesses or other selected groups such as churches, teenagers, retired people, housewives, etc., visit them and ask. You are guaranteed to learn something although you may not want to hear it. People love to point out to others why a business won't be successful.

After you have an indication of the market potential, you will want to incorporate some conservative sales figures into your business plan. This is the point at which most small businessmen overestimate the potential for their business.

In their enthusiasm they inflate potential sales volume through a sophisticated formula using desire, hope, inadequate research data, and raw courage as the variables. They leave out such essentials as the necessity for sales calls or advertising to increase sales. Somehow, they have latched on to that one product or service that is going to sell itself. After all, in their line of reasoning, everyone wants it or needs it. After convincing themselves that the projected sales will be there, they then refuse to believe their own estimates. They may crank in the overhead figures and somehow no profit shows up in the bottomline. The one thing they didn't forget to include was management salary. To rectify this unprofitable situation on paper they then work themselves back to the sales figures, adjust them upward appropriately, and "presto," they show a profitable enterprise. Full speed ahead!

The unfortunate aspect of such start-ups is that too many small businessmen are overly ambitious in the size of their start-up. Instead of minimal commitment in expenditures to test the waters, they match the size of their emotional commitment with financial commitment. The emotional commitment can quickly subside if projected sales volumes are not forthcoming, but the financial commitment is largely irrevocable.

- Keep your marketing research projections conservative and realistic.

- Ensure that your financial commitment to start-up operations is small and conservative. You can always expand operations later if revenues support it.

- Do not permit your emotional commitment to cause you to overestimate sales projections or overcommit your financial capabilities. You will need the emotional commitment but maintain a reserve there too. You will need it.

Expansion

Your business plan should provide for planned expansion. Many small businesses have a successful start-up and appear to be experiencing phenomenal growth. Then, suddenly, rumors of cash flow problems precede a spectacular bankruptcy. Doors close overnight and creditors swoop down to pick over the lean bones of the fallen victim. What could have happened? They seemed to have been doing so well.

Too-rapid expansion coupled with inadequate financial controls cause the demise of many small businesses. Growth is something for which virtually every business strives. If their start-up was successful and profitable, they reach out for an increasingly larger share of the market. In order to do this they must build the supporting structure. In their enthusiasm for growth they commit the same error many commit in a start-up. Too much of everything, except sales, too soon.

There are critical stages in the growth of every business that require new insights, new controls, and maybe even new management. Above all, growth requires cash and cost controls. Lose either one of those and you can lose the "bubble." Short term financing for small businesses can be helpful when expanding, as long as the pay-back can be supported by additional sales.

It is very difficult to increase cash reserves in a small business. Once the company starts exeriencing cash flow problems, they should abandon or defer expansion plans. Your business plans, both short and long range, should be based on a pay as you go, learn as you grow, basis.

FRANCHISES AND DISTRIBUTORSHIPS

There are literally hundreds of opportunities to buy franchises or distributorships. Every imaginable product and service is represented in offerings. There are so many people wanting your money while at the same time offering you a chance of a lifetime, that you wonder if you're the only one who is not making a million dollars. Testimonials attesting to successes in short periods of time clutter magazines. Business success and high earnings are awaiting those who act quickly. But just how good are some of these opportunities?

To be sure, there are success stories in both franchise operations and distributorships. However, the real questions you should ask yourself when looking into these offerings are numerous and serious business questions. If you don't know the questions to ask, get help or stay clear of the opportunity. The potential for both loss of your money and business failure in franchise operations and distributorships is great unless you know what you're doing. The sales pitch they offer can make it sound easy and highly profitable. Be aware that in most cases, for every success there are many failures.

Franchises

Franchise operations usually involve substantial investment. This investment can be anywhere from a low of about five thousands dollars to hundreds of thousands of dollars.

What does this type of investment buy you? In some cases, only the exclusive rights to represent and sell a product, service, or brand name in a specific, defined geographic area. In other cases, the cost for entry may include all arrangements of buying, leasing, or renting store frontage, initial inventory supplies, access to supply channels, operations training, bookkeeping services, and follow up support. Essentially, you pay for what you get. Low entry fee equals minimum support; high entry fee, hopefully, gains you full support.

Most states have specific laws relating to the minimum duties a franchisor must perform for the franchisee. Those laws help regulate franchising operations. However, you cannot always depend on them protecting your rights even if you know what they are. It is difficult in court to support a claim of insufficient support when there is a minimum measure of support being provided.

The best approach when dealing with a franchising operation is to spend the necessary money to have a lawyer and a CPA examine the prospectus and give you their independent evaluations of the opportunity. The cost for their advice may be the best investment you ever make. Don't assume you have the knowledge required to come to a sound business decision with the information provided to you by the franchisor. The legal and financial ramifications are too great to assume anything. Your lawyer and CPA will be able to ask those hard questions which can mean the difference between you investing in the business or taking a "bye" on the opportunity.

You should never feel that by consulting a lawyer or a CPA you're showing ignorance or inadequate business acumen. There would be far fewer business failures if they were consulted when things started to turn sour. They perform an essential service to businesses.

Usually businessmen wait until things go wrong before they consult a lawyer or CPA. By then the damage is done and money is lost. Even if the franchisor supplies you with legal and financial advice, contract for an independent evaluation by your own lawyer and CPA. You're dealing in money and your future -- protect yourself.

In any franchise operation you must ask yourself if the opportunity really represents what you want to do. Don't think only about the money that supposedly can be made. You may not like what you have to do to make it a viable operation. There is virtually no franchise operation in which you can expect to be an absentee owner unless the investment is very large, or it already is a profitable concern. Otherwise, you will have to do the work yourself.

The franchisor is not giving you the opportunity out of the goodness of his heart. He expects to make money. Some of it he makes from your initial investment; the rest he makes in a percentage of the gross sales volume. Note, **gross sales** — not net profit. That means that you must pay **all** overhead expenses out of the gross sales volume remaining. That includes any salary you expect to take out of the enterprise.

If you have the money to invest, a good franchise operation can offer you the potential for quick start-up in a proven market. The name and reputation of the company can bring you volume business quickly. The experience in operations they share with you can reduce the number of problems that you may otherwise have in operating the business. Talk to any of the original McDonald's Hamburger franchisees and you can appreciate how successful a franchise operation can be.

The thing to remember is that the franchisor will be raking off a portion of the gross sales volume from your opening day through eternity, unless you have a buy out agreement. Even if an equity position is offered, he may also be entitled to a share of the net profits. **READ THE CONTRACT CAREFULLY** and **HAVE YOUR LAWYER AND CPA LOOK IT OVER.** That advice cannot be stressed strongly enough.

The other thing to consider before you buy a franchise is the alternative of starting your own business. If you have the money to invest, why not do it yourself and be the sole owner? If it is a success, you may very well be selling franchises to others.

Distributorships

There are hundreds of different types of distributorships being offered by virtually all types of companies. Some require very high entry fees. Automobiles, heavy equipment, beer, electronics equipment, and a host of other products offer solid business opportunities for those who can afford them and understand their market. Working our way down from these high ticket items we encounter a stifling array of products and services for which distributorships are offered.

Just how good are distributorships? What can they offer? Again, it is the success stories that excite us and enable companies that offer distributorships to attract tens of thousands of people to their ranks.

Among the distributorships are well known operations that are avidly worked by everyone from housewives and secretaries to your boss or his children. In some cases, the products are excellent. So excellent in fact, that it seems you cannot go to work, attend a meeting, or visit a friend without being approached to either buy their products or sign up as a distributor. That makes for tough competition and success will be hard earned. Are you aggressive enough to compete in such a market?

The primary thing you should understand about distributorships is that they require sales work. There is absolutely no way you will escape that necessity. So, if sales work is not your forte, stay clear of distributorships. Your chances for success in a distributorship without sales work will be very limited indeed.

Any distributor can portray a marketing plan which, when successfully executed, can generate fantastic dollar volumes for the hardworking distributor. In theory the plan works and some people have made it work well. The two essential ingredients for success are superior salesmanship and a great deal of hard sales work. Having the right product certainly helps but salesmanship is more important. Contrary to the promotional literature that some distributorships have, people will not beat a path to your doorstep to purchase the product. More likely, you will be the one who is beating a path to hundreds of doorsteps trying to get people to buy the product or sign up as distributors themselves.

There is no denying the fact that some people have made fine salaries, even a million dollars, on distributorships. Those who have made a million were on the ground floor of the start-up with a good product. They entered a marketing scheme which capitalizes on the multiplicative effect of each distributor signing up ever more distributors until they are getting an override on the production of hundreds, or even thousands, of other distributors. The power of these marketing schemes is staggering, both in terms of volume of product sold as well as income to those who really work at it. For every success, though, there are many who end up with a closet or garage full of unsold products.

The things to watch out for are:

- Entry fee
- Demand for product
- Competition in product line
- Exclusivity of territory

If the entry fee is low, as in the case of buying a sample sales kit for a nominal sum, you may want to try selling it. Just don't invest in a lot of the product with the hope of selling it. You may find out it's a lot harder to sell than you thought. You may also discover that the profits for the time and effort make it a marginally worthwhile endeavor.

Beware of the requirement that you invest thousands of dollars for a heavy inventory of the product at the onset, regardless of the mark up you can put on the sale. Ask yourself the following questions:

- "What am I going to do with all this product if I can't sell it?"

- "Has the company given me an unconditional guarantee, in writing, that they will buy back the product for what I paid for it, if I cannot sell it?"

Don't take anyone's word regarding demand for the product. Try selling some of it yourself. Don't permit the lure of potential earnings to cloud the reality that you must do hard sales work in order to make any money, much less a lot of money.

If there is a similar product on the market, how well does this product compete. Again, try selling some of it so **you know** its potential.

If you're unable to get, in writing, exclusive rights to a territory, expect everyone and his brother to be competing against you if the product is any good.

Distributorships can be profitable. Just don't invest any sizeable amount of cash in one unless you really know what you're doing. It is easy to get caught up in the excitement of potential earnings, believing that you have what it takes to make a success out of it. If you had a dollar for everyone who tried a distributorship and ended up with a closet or garage full of unsold products, you could retire today.

The list of products sold through distributorships is endless. There are flower pots, cameras, cosmetics, protein powder, vitamins, paints, pictures, smoke alarms, office supplies and auto accessories and literally hundreds of other products and services. Each of them attract hundreds, and even thousands to their ranks. Perhaps the best way to approach such opportunities is to try it with a limited investment on a part-time basis. If one is successful for you, then and only then will you want to make a 100 percent commitment to it. Just remember, you will work hard for what you earn.

SUMMARY

Many people have fulfilled the dream of owning their own business. The independence and earning potential of owning a business are attractive incentives to those desiring to do so. Whatever your motivation is to start a business, that motivation must be backed by a firm commitment to succeed in the face of any adversity in order to stay viable in business. A good business plan is essential to success. That plan should address the essentials of capitalization, financial controls, market research, and expansion planning.

Franchises and distributorships should be approached with caution. Their advertised potential causes many people to enter into them with scant knowledge of what is really required to be successful. Unless you clearly enjoy sales work and are prepared to make a commitment to hard work in order to succeed, it is probably best to stay clear of them.

Before you invest a sizeable amount of money in any business, have your lawyer and CPA give their evaluation of the opportunity. The fee you pay for their services may very well end up being your best investment.

ENCOURAGEMENT

Business opportunities abound in America. With sound planning, you can be successful in your own business.

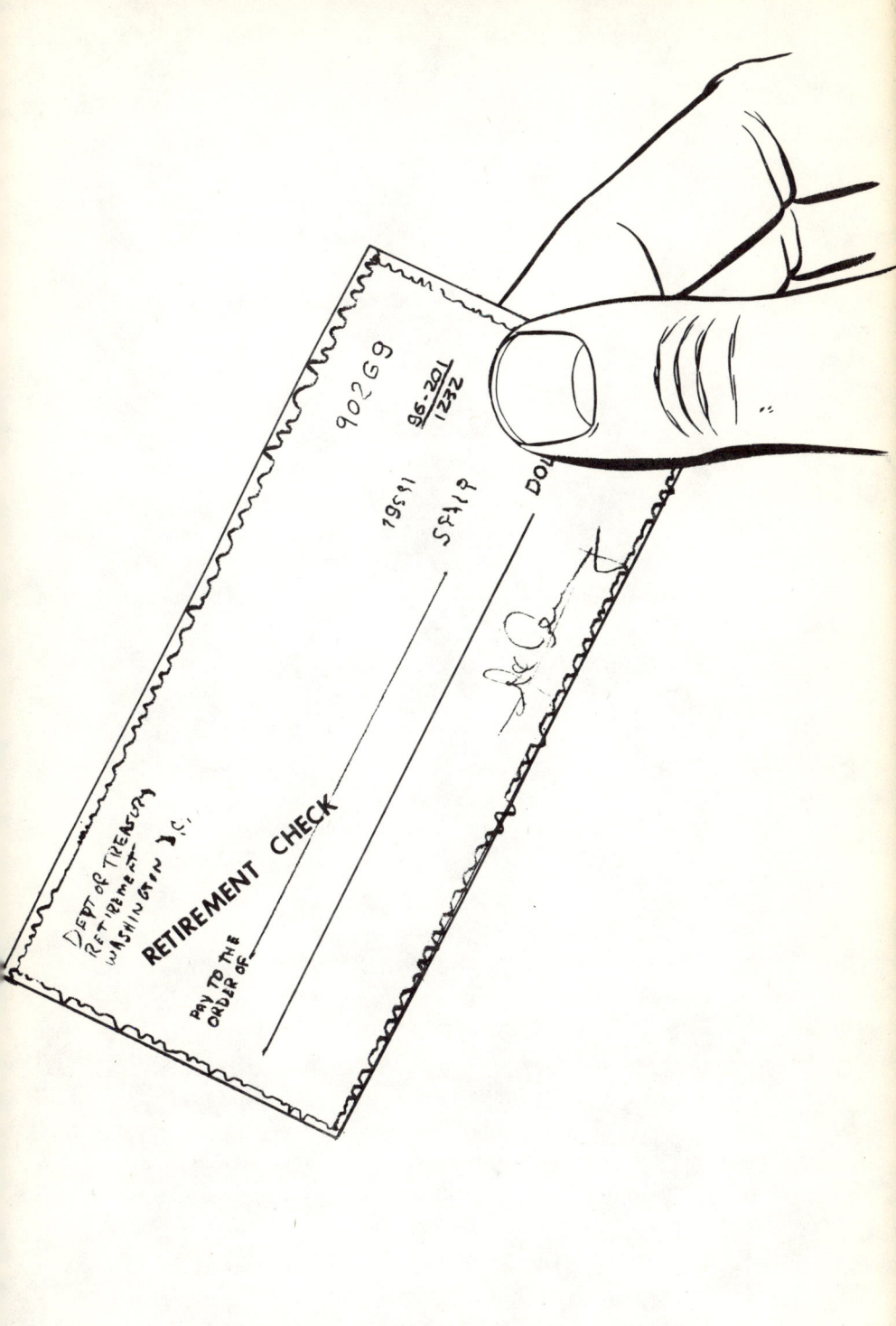

Chapter 15

THE CASE FOR STAYING IN

INTRODUCTION

For those people in the military who are considering leaving (except for retirement) there is a strong case for staying in until retirement. In support of this view, consider what others who have left before retirement have to say, as well as those who have remained in until they retired.

I SHOULD HAVE

There is scarcely a day that goes by that the military retiree doesn't have some former serviceman say to him, "I wish I would have stayed in. I'd be retired now." As the former military person approaches age 50 or 60, he realizes what little security he really has for his approaching retirement years. There are very few companies that approach the retirement benefits of Federal Civil Service or military service. Even if the employee has sufficient longevity to realize a retirement benefit, he must often wait until a certain age to start collecting it.

Because of the inflation we have been experiencing during the past decade, many people who retired on fixed incomes have found it necessary to re-enter the job market in order to make ends meet. They have no built-in cost-of-living raises in their retirement plan.

As they look back over the years, they realize how fast time went by and how little they accomplished toward gaining financial independence. They realize, too, that the hardships and discipline they had to endure on the job during the past 20 or more years were no less than they would have encountered had they remained in the military. Their refrain is common: "I wish I would have stayed in. I'd be retired now."

They still face years of labor in a job market that discriminates against them because of their age. If they didn't gain success before now, the chances of an employer giving them the opportunity are slim. They look back to their years in the military as an opportunity lost. They let it pass for trite reasons when considered in the light of today's economic realities. Too late they realized the wisdom of sticking it out in the military to retirement.

HAPPY I DID

When a military retiree enters the job market, he quickly realizes what he has in his military retirement. Men his own age do not have anywhere near the measure of his security. They see how shallow the long term benefits are in the company they work for.

They can look back on their military career with a sense of pride, accomplishment and success. They have a lifetime of rich experiences about which they can reminisce. In addition to retaining many of the privileges they had while they were on active duty, they know where their next paycheck is coming from. They may not be able to live on it in the style to which they have become accustomed, but it ensures that life will be easier. Retirees consider their 20 or more years of service a sound investment which will continue to pay them dividends.

THE CHOICE IS YOURS

Of course, the choice to stay in the military or re-enter civilian life is completely yours. Hopefully, this book will help make the transition from military service to civilian employment easier for you if you choose to re-enter civilian life.